HIGHER EDUCATION IN BLACKNESS;

A DILEMMA

HIGHER EDUCATION IN BLACKNESS;
A DILEMMA

J.R. GLOVER

iUniverse

HIGHER EDUCATION IN BLACKNESS; A DILEMMA

iUniverse books may be ordered through booksellers or by contacting:

iUniverse
1663 Liberty Drive
Bloomington, IN 47403
www.iuniverse.com
1-800-Authors (1-800-288-4677)

ISBN: 978-1-4917-6145-8 (sc)
ISBN: 978-1-4917-6146-5 (e)

Print information available on the last page.

iUniverse rev. date: 03/04/2015

This book is written in memory of my deceased wife of 46 years, Hattie, my deceased mother Marcella Harris and my current wife Wendy

CONTENTS

CONTENTS

FOREWORD

It was not very long ago that there were no college educated family members or friends in most of our black neighborhoods or communities. Most of this was attributed to a lack of financing as well as a lack of opportunities. Blacks simply couldn't afford it! Had it not been for the G.I. Bill which was available to military veterans in the 60's, I would not have been able to get a college education. Today things have changed somewhat, and many of our families have now produced college graduates. However, everything that shines is not gold.

The purpose of this writing is to raise awareness of a significant problem facing the black community and the educational process which I define as a dilemma. This affects the cultural relations between the black and white communities of America. In many ways this is a subtle and often unforeseen situation that escapes the attention of those unaware. We as people are often prone to focus our attention on matters that concern our own immediate lives and families.

The concern here, however, is focused on this subtle and seemingly insignificant issue that has now, over the years, grown to crisis proportions in the black community. We as blacks today often don't understand it ourselves, because more blacks than ever are getting college educations, and this is causing a false sense of euphoria among us, because little or no change is taking place in our culture, similar to that of the first black president in America, Barack Obama!

We need to stay on guard of progress accomplished in some areas of modern life today, which tend to minimize the reality that every time we take one step forward, we often take one step backwards as well. This is what the 50th anniversary of the march on Washington that is celebrated now in 2013 has taught us. In spite of the gains made in racial relations between blacks and whites, Martin Luther King, Junior's dream has yet to be realized in its entirety.

Ironically, there is now a crisis of **Self Identity** among blacks today called "**blackness**," which is threatening to undermine the black community, and the importance of history specifically of how black Americans have struggled to identify themselves in white America over the years.

This has become such an issue, that even whites do not know how to address blacks by name, for fear of saying the wrong thing or reference. Even the Census tracts of the U.S. have various listings for blacks by racial identification.

The extent of this problem is seen more clearly through the eyes of a black American who has lived and experienced the events depicted in this writing, as well as continuing to experience them even today. This is important for the mere fact that a black male is the one who needs to write these accounts, as they contain issues of a sensitive nature as well as critique of black lifestyle, that only a black college educated male can espouse from first-hand experience!

Blacks, especially males, who have successfully graduated from college, often have negative experiences with their peers because of it in the community in which they live. This has become so prevalent today, that young black Americans who attend college are often ridiculed by their classmates, if they study long hours in school, often ignoring the many" after hour activities" in the dorms and on the college campus, and are also belittled in their communities as losing their "blackness" or becoming "whitewashed."

James R. Glover

INTRODUCTION

First, let us begin our discussion by talking about education in general. We all know that going to school and receiving an education is required of all citizens as a legal obligation. In elementary, middle school, and high school, it is **mandatory** that all children and youth go to school. We are not required to graduate or complete our education, unfortunately, which remains a mystery to me as to why one would not finish school, unless it is because of severe financial hardship or health conditions within the family.

The crux of the problem is better understood as the result of a personal agenda or mindset that dictates the desires and ambitions of the individual, no matter what others wish for them. This is probably one of the most frustrating concerns for parents to deal with involving their children, who always want what is best for their child, but often are unable to make it happen.

You can lead a horse to water, but you can't make him drink. This axiom is true not only for the horse, but to kids in school as well. This is a matter of what is of utmost importance to the child, and to a great extent of how they were raised. Because of this truism, they are made to go to school which, unfortunately does not mean that they will become students, with the desire to learn and become educated. Many students become **in school dropouts** simply because they choose not to become educated, or who fail to see the need of an education.

Periodically this time away from home by kids, however, is seen as an opportunity by some irresponsible parents to have "free" time. This is so unfortunate! If blame is to be place anywhere, it must begin with the parents of these children, who even when they have the time, do not help their children with Home Work, or talk to them about the importance or purpose or how education can affect their lives. In my opinion, this is precisely where the breakdown begins!

Society cannot be blamed for the shortcomings of parents, which some sociologist often attempt to use, as an excuse or scapegoat in many situations, but instead is often the result of parents who themselves have not received a college education, and therefore do not see the necessity to emphasize this to their children. It is indeed remarkable how we as parents often pass down the principles of our own upbringing to our children.

A child basically learns by being taught, or by example. If parents have a lackadaisical attitude about education, the children will have one as well. The family unit is the single most important fabric of any society. The attitude concerning education seems to have been placed on the individual, rather than on the family group.

I believe that this dates back to the 60's and 70's during the time of the social revolution in this country, where the decision making was placed on the **individual** rather than society as a whole, which was an excuse for it! That is why it pains me so much today to see how our government is undermining the family unit today, by placing so many proscriptions on parents when it comes to raising their children!

Society cannot dictate morality or parental supervision of children as matters of law, as it attempts to do by such actions of CSB (children services board). No child is greater than the parent. However, this appears to be the direction that our government is headed in. If you take a close look at the laws being passed down, even by the Supreme Courts, it is almost being weighted on the side of the children.

Children are no longer required to get parental permission concerning abortions, and obtaining contraceptives. Yet they claim that it is the parent's obligation to talk to their children and educate them about sexual morality and the subsequent responsibility that it entails. What is that, if it not a double standard with mixed messages?

Children can now receive counseling and intervention on matters of sex from Planned Parenthood without parental consent. I cannot help but believe that Planned Parenthood from its inception was designed to **complement** the family unit, rather than to divide it as the current practice has done. It was designed to be an extension to parental upbringing, much the same as the original intent of CSB (Children's Services Board), which, unfortunately has recently undergone a complete metamorphosis.

To complicate matters even further, as hard as it is to believe, children can now **Divorce** their parents in a court of law if you can believe that! I confess that I do not know all of the circumstances in this situation, but just to ascertain such a notion under **any circumstance is absurd.** An underage child can even get an abortion without parental consent.

Children are children and parents are parents! You cannot reverse the roles. This does not mean that children do not have rights. Of course they do, but as children! When CSB is given the authority to dictate how a child is raised by their parents, this violates its original intention. This is not entirely the fault of CSB. As a society, we have blurred the distinction between discipline and child abuse.

Discipline is becoming a thing of the past as our society no longer is capable of distinguishing between family chastisement done in love, and child abuse! For example if a child goes to school with whelps on his or her legs from a belt or switch, the teacher or counselor are told to report such things to the school principle. In order to protect the school from possible legal action, the principle or teacher then reports it to CSB, who can then come into the home and remove the child for **suspected** child abuse.

Children are very astute in picking up on the dichotomy of playing one side against the other. They learn at an early age how to pit the father against the mother, and vice versa, in order to get their way. The problem with the government's intervention in parental rights is the erosion of the family unit. The problem with this approach is that it does not extend to just discipline, but to a host of other factors which ties the parent's hands.

For example, when a time old phrases used by our parents in disciplining us as their children "I brought you into the world, and I can take you out," or "if you keep mouthing off, you'll pick your teeth up off the floor," are now being interpreted as **verbal abuse**! If that's the case, all of our parents who raised us in times past, would be in jail! Common sense will tell you that loving parents do not mean these expressions literally, but are only using them metaphorically. How can you raise a child without an accessional threat of consequence?

Even the Bible teaches that the wages of sin is death! Is Jesus then accused of verbal abuse? When a child is disciplined in love, they know that when it happens, it is because of something that they deserved. I remembered the words of my mother as she disciplined me "this hurts as me as much as it hurts you." Does that means that either she was lying or being deceptive? I didn't understand it at the time, but now I know exactly what she meant.

It is difficult enough to discipline your child, but without it your child will grow up not able to tell right from wrong. And that is one of the biggest problems with our children today. If we remember raising our children, they learn how to play one parent against the other at an early age. If a child cannot get what he or she wants from one parent, they will go to the other to get their way.

This ploy is now being played out not only in the home, but in society, when our children know that they now **divorce** their parents in court. These types of laws and regulations only serve to undermine the family unit!

Children are able to pick up on this, thus rendering their parents almost powerless to impose discipline in the home. If the parents of the 50's and 60's were alive today rearing their children, 75% of them would be in jail! Even when a parent today threaten their children with phrases like "I brought you into this world, and I can take you out," which are only words, they are accused of **verbal** abuse.

You can't Have your cake your cake and eat it too. Children also intimidate school principals and teachers with threats of violence themselves, when it comes to being paddled or corrected in school for undesirable behavior and conduct in the classroom, and they know how to play the system. This is why it is necessary in many of our schools to have police cars and metal detectors as a means of supplying security because of a lack of discipline!

To paddle a child today is considered **corporal punishment!** What a misnomer! Capital punishment is the electric chair or life imprisonment, not a spanking! Any society that cannot tell the difference is in serious trouble. I completely sympathize with principals and teachers who are powerless to discipline their students. Because of the disruption within the family unit by government intervention, teachers spend almost as much time being surrogate parents, than in teaching their students!

When you couple this with spending more time over these concerns than you do with teaching, which is what the job description is for, added to the low salary that most teachers are paid as professionals, no wonder the morale is low and the work unsatisfying. Don't just take my word for it, talk to school teachers yourself!

This means that in many ways, teachers and schools must assume a role that was not anticipated in their training. Much the same as nurses in hospitals now are now being asked to do the work that nurse aids or orderly's used to do. This simply means that they spend more time than necessary doing menial tasks that they were not trained to do in school. Likewise when the educational system does not meet superimposed standards by society, the school system is somehow to blame.

This in its own right is simply another example of blaming the victim, as it was practiced in race relations in the 70's when blacks were accused of being responsible for their conditions, as it they were Self Imposed.

However, **secondary** education, beyond that which is required by law is a voluntary elective for the adult individual. The primary purpose of secondary education is to learn how to become an individual **critical** thinker, able to function on your own, by learning how to disseminate information into an internal and logical system of understanding! This creates a mature adult no longer dependent upon being told what to believe and how.

We are taught that education is the key to success, and while this may be true for white Americans, it has not been the case for blacks. This is what leads to the finger pointing and taunts by blacks of other blacks..."I told you so, that's the white man's ideology!" Rather than understanding education as being the key to success, it should be understood instead as the betterment of the individual! Success is a relative and ambiguous term, often delineated along racial and ethnic lines.

Because of this disparity, education has borne the brunt of discrimination, deception, purposeful misinformation, and a host of other fallacies, that has led modern day black militants to create the present dilemma that we are faced with today. Somehow they have been successful in creating the illusion that education is a tool used by white society to mislead black American by the phrase of being "whitewashed."

Since when has learning taken on a white, black connotation anyway? This particular dilemma has existed for over a hundred years or so, and has now evolved into a cultural systemic condition, that has polarized our society as never before. The genesis of this situation will be examined in detail later, and is not intended to place blame on any one particular individual or group, but rather to see more clearly what our past practices as a society have brought to light on this issue.

Those of us today are not responsible for this situation as we have inherited the problem. However, we are none the less responsible for its solution! This responsibility is to be equally shared by both groups involved, black or white. It is time for black Americans to stop making excuses for our own shortcomings, caused by the racial inequalities of the past, though valid to a degree, and for whites to stop blaming the victims of these past discriminations, as somehow being responsible for their own demise. Finger pointing is for children, while solutions to problems are for adults!

As strange as it may seem, especially for us blacks who have gone on to a degree in higher education, as many of us have been encouraged to do by parents and friends, education and the black community are strange fellows! Often they don't seem to fit together, and this is not only a tragedy, but an oxymoron which defies a logical explanation. It is the odd couple!

Ask any black American if they believe that education is a valuable possession to have, and the overwhelming answer will be "yes." Yet this illogical dichotomy exists nonetheless, and is very visible in the black community, and becoming increasingly prevalent among the young blacks today, especially the black male. Why you might ask, does this blatant contradiction exist?

The failure to co-exist between education and the advancement of Black Americans is not only unnatural, but an Oxymoron, a mystery that is hard to understand or fathom. At best it is an unhealthy relationship that can only lead to a further decline as a race, and on a larger scale, as a nation.

Many blacks do not want to own up to this problem, and many would like to sweep it under the rug, but avoidance is only a coward's way out. Turning one's head or looking the other way is not the answer! Knowing the illness is half of the cure. We as blacks at least need to face up this problem, which is rapidly becoming a crisis.

There is often a defiant attitude in the black community surrounding higher education, which is often perceived as somehow threatening our black identity. Some of our black people have a sense that in order to safeguard who and what we are as black people, we need to be skeptical of white indoctrination and influences which tend to undermine our sense of "**blackness.**"

When pressured to explain exactly what the essence of blackness is, you get no satisfactory explanation. It's as if every person has their own interpretation. But without an acceptable definition, you have only opinions, and opinions are like eyes in normal persons, everyone has at least two.

Let's struggle to understand this phenomenon of the black's sense of self preservation. Does being labeled as black, mean that we need to talk black? When educated black people speak fluent and correct English, rather than the ghetto or slang language that prevails in the average black community, they are said to have lost their **blackness.**

A brief look at the recent past will help to highlight this problem. We all remember the only black man to become a Supreme Court judge, Clarence Thomas. Aside from being republican that did not endear him to blacks, one of the biggest criticisms of him in the black community was that he didn't talk like a black man! He was articulate and very well spoken in spite of his political ideologies.

Another example can be seen in General Colin Powell, the former Chief of Staff of the United States. While he was very respected and looked up to in the black community, he was not really accepted as a true black man for many of the same reasons mentioned above in Clarence Thomas.

Another example of an educated, articulate, and beloved black man is the popular figure of Bill Cosby. He is generally viewed as one who speaks very intelligently and insightfully, but did not share many of the views of urban blacks. His outspoken criticism of many black philosophies and practices is seen as being too white.

Still another example is that of Tiger Woods, who refused to be labeled as an African American, which of course he was not, being of mixed heritage. His mother was Taiwanese, and his father black. In my own family, we are mixed with black and Cherokee Indian (as my great grandmother was a full blooded Cherokee), therefore I am not African American in the true sense of the word, but still consider myself a black American.

So what then is true blackness? The word "Blackness" therefore begs the question of a true definition. Blacks have a habit of referring to blackness as "**keeping it real**." What precisely does that mean?

Does keeping it real mean that one must accept the way of inner city life, and its high crime rate that is a major part of it? How then is black on black crime, gang affiliations and killing, a part of keeping it real? Does it mean that one must accept young black parents leaving their children to be raised by their grandparents, aunts and uncles, while not attending school functions with their children, such as PTA meetings, Science Fairs, and open house?

Does it mean that one must accept some persons that intentionally use poor and lazy speech habits while talking, or having a sullen attitude and facial expression while doing so?

Critiquing the term:

It appears that the true definition and understanding of "blackness" is more than just a term or label but a reality! Upon examination, it appears that the meaning of the term is left up to the individual using it! If one's identity and individuality is dependent upon an expression or term, then that individual has no **personhood** to call their own.

We are created with a unique character, and personality unlike any other. How we view ourselves should be one of an individual's Self Understanding. Sometimes, as blacks, we have an identity crisis as to who and what we are according to how others refer to us as.

Back in the day when blacks were referred to by the "N" word (niggers),which would always invoked a fighting response from blacks as though the word was true, displayed an attitude of identifying ourselves by the label. I have been confronted by young blacks negatively, even today, for preferring to be called a black American, rather than as an African American.

I am Jim Glover no matter what name I'm labeled with, and by what I'm called. I know **who I am and what I am! One thing that I remember very well as a child that my mother taught me was "the only way that someone is better than you is that they are a better person!"**

When name calling is allowed to illicit a predetermined response, it is a form of behavioral control! As long as whites could predict a certain response by the use of the word, it demonstrated as measure of control.

When blacks finally realized this, they responded by saying that the "N" word according to the dictionary is "**trash", and could also be applied to their own family members as well. This is how the value of an education and the expansion of knowledge, enhances one's understanding!**

Other than the color of one's skin, the most definable way to identify a black person is by their speech. When you talk on the telephone, in most cases you can identify the person as an African American by their diction, voice tone or use of the English language.

The latter is sometimes an **embarrassment** even among blacks, when listening to how some stumble and falter in their expressions. I don't know how many times that I have cringed when listening to blacks doing interviews, often not completing sentences or thoughts.

This is not an affront on those who lack a proper education, which I personally find no excuse for since primary education is free, but it sometimes make you wonder if some of these persons don't intentionally do this some of the time. It often appears as a way to express their blackness, or at least a contrived means of expression.

If it is intentional to some degree, it points to the vast separation of the white and black communities.

This may be offensive to some blacks, but the truth must be told. The manner in which we speak is often a clear reflection of the extent of our education! This is so obvious that you can often tell which side of town a person is from simply by the way they speak! Whenever I listen to a black doing an interview with good diction and use of the English language, it makes me proud! The axiom that words are power is true, because it often reflects on a person's character, which is the best way to sell and represent oneself to others.

As a matter of fact, many times we are judged by others simply by the way we speak, as well as our body language and posture! Failure to make eye contact when talking is a pretty good indication of a lack of self Confidence and intimacy. First impressions are the most lasting, and many times we don't get a second chance.

When I interviewed candidates for employment years ago as a department head in the firm that I worked for, there were certain signs that I looked for during the interview that would immediately eliminate some individuals for consideration to be hired.

One of the primary signs was posture and body language. If a candidate slouched down in his seat while sitting in an interview, they had already begun to dig a hole for themselves because it demonstrated a lazy attitude and character. If a candidate came to an interview with his hair unkempt and an Afro Pick sticking in it, they were automatically eliminated.

I use this expression to the younger generation as a learning example! Thirdly, if a candidate lit up a cigarette without first getting permission to do so, was an example of presumptuousness and disrespect.

Another example was a preoccupation with the salary attached to the position. There is nothing wrong with wanting to know what a position paid, but it's the timing of the question about it that is critical. If it comes too early in the interview, it's an indication that money is probably more important than the position itself.

As an example, at a job interview, the manner in which you present yourself is one of the single most important factors in impressing your interviewee. Often by just talking, you can give the appearance that you know more than you actually do. My philosophy when doing a job interview was always that if I get as far as the interview, the job was mine! This proved to be true more times than not! Words are indeed power, which coined the phrase "the pen is mightier than the sword."

I believe that the focus on the way a person talks created the movement by blacks to formulate **Ebonics,** as a failed attempt to cover up these deficiencies in speech, by attempting to establish it as a type of **counter** language, to the extent that there was a movement afoot for a while to have it recognized as a valid form of language. This is not to be confused with the slang words of the fifties and sixties, which were limited to a select group of expressions known as "cool." Let's not confuse apples and oranges!

This attempt went beyond dialect, which is a regionalized speaking **accent,** such as Midwest, Appalachian, Southern, New England, etc., to the formulation of an **alternative** language to be formally recognized. This attempt was clearly a cultural protest of separation

Does being "black" mean you have a certain manner in which to dress? If you notice a counter culture of dress popular among black males today, is the practice of wearing their pants below their hips, showing their underwear in public, which is considered to be disrespectful by both blacks and whites. If you don't walk around showing your underwear, and holding up your pants with one hand as if belts do not exist, and wearing your pants two sizes too big, then you're not being black?

I have yet to figure out what is wrong with custom made clothes, or buying clothes that fit your size. Nice fitting clothes are not only fashionable, but neat. I imagine that wearing clothes that fit is a symbol of the white way of dressing. If I'm wrong, someone needs to tell me how I am? We've all heard the expression that it is not what is on your back that counts, but what is in your heart that matters.

This current way of dressing by young black males today appears to be a reflection of the influence of gang culture and rappers. What it intends to signify is beyond this black writer! I know that dress styles changed from generation to generation, but it's still true that you are generally judged by your appearance, because it is a reflection of your personality and character.

When you see a person who is covered with an inordinate amount of body piercings, and spiked hair for example, you automatically form an opinion about his or her character. This is a normal human reaction to appearances. Be this as it may, it is unfortunate that these factors have affected the nature of education within the black community in a negative way. If a student is fully committed to study, they are called "book worms or nerds."

For every situation in life, there is genesis or a beginning. The failure to have a close relationship between higher education and being black in America is no exception. This condition did not come overnight, and catch us unawares. Such is the case in point. Let's now examine this in close detail, as this situation has history that needs to be explored in order to be better understood.

CHAPTER ONE

1. The crisis in historical perspective

Every event has its origin or beginning. The root of this particular problem has its beginning in slavery and the subsequent events that followed. During the time of slavery, the slaves were considered as a sub human species, not fully human in all respects. By creating this irrational **myth** as a means of justifying the practice of slavery, proof texting of the Bible was done as well. This practice led to the false belief that somehow the separation of the races was ordained by God.

However, here lies the problem that this work addresses with the youth of today and the current culture. In many ways they operate in a vacuum of knowledge and history, which tends to eliminate the cutting edge of the problem. The youth of today are basically unaware of the historical issues that have created this dilemma. All they know is that somehow a college degree does not seem to fit comfortably in the black community.

They are unaware of the rhetoric of the 60's and 70's which labeled getting a college education as a means of "whitewashing" the black culture into the mainstream of the white American way of thinking, according to some early black militant thought. This will be discussed a little later in more detail when we address the issue of "**blackness**" today and how it affects higher education.

We as black intellectuals today and parents as well, have done a poor job in educating our youth today as to why this dilemma exists and its origin. They will not learn about this situation in school, because most whites do not know this problem exists in the black community, and many blacks themselves are unaware of the problem, or choose to ignore it or turn the other cheek in apathy and resignation.

Part of this problem may be due to families and parents who do not have going to college as part of the family structure and therefore is not on their radar screen. If a family has never had a college graduate in it, then it can become something that is unintentionally overlooked or not considered.

When some black college students ridicule other classmates about taking their education too seriously, or becoming '"book worms," it is only a reflection of this problem. Unless you are a college student or a professor, you may not know that this problem of belittling one another is practiced among black college students.

Just ask those who know and they will tell you. What sense does it make to be a college student, and then criticize those who work hard to achieve it? Yet this goes on in our universities among our black students who carry this street mentality into their classrooms.

This kind of conduct clearly exhibits a kind of paranoia and unbalanced thinking. The scary thing about it is that it happens quite often unconsciously or intentionally. It is a reflexive action many times without prior aforethought or intention. If you ask the person doing this as to why, you will probably not get a satisfactory answer other than "we're just trying to get so and so straightened out, and get their head screwed on right."

This is where the danger comes in when we do things without knowing why they're done. Much of the racism practiced today is done in much the same manner. It is a taught and accepted systemic reality that is no longer simply a black and white issue. Many people and religions today harbor racial prejudices hid under the umbrella of scriptural and biblical misinterpretations. This practice is termed proof texting, and is one of the key ingredients of Jim Crow laws that existed for so long.

Proof texting

For the reader who is not familiar with the practice of biblical proof texting, it is the practice of taking isolated passages of scripture out of its proper context, and making it say what the reader wants it to say in order to justify a certain position. This is commonly done by various church denominations over doctrinal beliefs, as well as world leaders to justify their position on a certain issue, as President Ronald Reagan did in the 60's relative to nuclear proliferation (Luke 14: 28-31).

How the practice of racism was able to survive for so long, is a complete mystery, seeing that it had no basis in logical reasoning or scripture. Racism and prejudice are illogical concepts to begin with! Many people bought into this notion which validated the formation of hate groups such as the Klu Klux Klan (KKK], which hid behind the cloak of religion (God intended that the races should be separate), as well as the radical groups of Islam (suicide bombings). Both religious groups should have spoken out against these forms of proof texting from the very outset!

If you are successful in attaching religious significance to any ideology that you espouse, it has the tendency tp endure for extended periods of time, because religious beliefs are the most difficult of anything to change or alter.

The existence of proof texting can only exist because of a lack of personal and corporate understanding of the religious texts concerned, which I deem in my companion work (The Art of Home Bible Study) as the **Pathology of Biblical infancy**, stemming from a lack of personal and corporate scriptural knowledge of the individuals concerned.

This is a prime example of the axiom that no enemy is greater than ignorance. An Infant knows no more than what they are taught, and therefore they depend upon everything they are told. Many of the world's problems today exist solely because decisions made by many of the world leaders go unchallenged, and because of a lack of mature and adult thinking on the behalf of too many individuals.

This lack of knowledge is what creates the **dependent learner,** who relies on what others tell them what the scriptures say. This kind of dependency is dangerous because it reflects the mindset of a child who relies on others to determine the direction of his or her life. This is why false prophets in Christianity such as Jimmy Jones, can lead people to commit suicide, and radical Islamic leaders can convince followers to do suicide bombings.

No matter how angry and upset things like this make us, if we are part of the ones stuck in ignorant bliss, we can blame no one but ourselves. We as a society have only ourselves to blame for allowing the inhumane treatment of minorities and women over the past decades to exist. We cannot blame the government, because we are the government!

When you hear people say things like the government needs to take control, they are attempting to shift the blame for their own inadequacies, to that of another source which doesn't exist. If we the people are the government, then **government** control cannot exist apart from each person!

Hypocrisy in practice

The persistent labeling and mindset of the **myth of inferiority** concerning blacks have come over centuries of indoctrination based on ignorance. Let's go back just sixty years ago, with the segregation of the armed forces and professional athletics in America. First let's begin with the segregated military, which consisted of all white units and all black units, because blacks were considered to be less capable of soldiering, and not as fit for service as their white constituents.

A prime example of this was the formation of the Tuskegee Institute, in which all black commissioned officers were not allowed to fly with white pilots in World War Two, because of being perceived as inferior, despite having the same educational background and flying ability as whites.

Can you imagine the disillusionment and frustration of these men who met all of the required criteria laid out before them, only to be told that it was not enough! The stigma suffered by these blacks left scars that have yet to heal, and have not been forgotten. This only recently came to light to our younger generation with the movie **Red Tails**. This docudrama serves as a vital and significant historical piece of information!

I myself served in the United States Marine Corp in the early sixties, before I realized that it was the last of the armed forces branch of service to integrate. I was the brunt of many racial slurs and bigotry during my enlistment which I paid little or no attention to, because it was a way of life during this time, and was generally accepted by the blacks of that time as normal. Unfortunately we are all victims of the time in which we live.

I was initially not cognizant of this racism because my primary purpose as a marine was to fight to defend my country and our freedom. That's why I can identify with the mindset of the Tuskegee airmen. However, during the Viet Nam conflict, hundreds of black marines fought and died for the United States of America, with little or no appreciation by the American public, including many whites as well.

The residual effects of these kinds of events leave permanent scars and hurts. Just look at the victims of the Viet Nam war some fifty years or so later. They still shed tears when they visit the wall in Washington D.C. commemorating the loss of their comrades. Many today still have not successfully reentered the mainstream of American society, and suffer from mental, psychological and sociological problems. Many of these were **white** veterans!

I clearly remember the time when I was eight years old over 60 years ago, when me and three brothers and sisters were downtown in Columbus, Ohio with our mother, when we were turned away from a department store that my mother had frequented for years, when they first opened up a cafeteria in the store to serve shoppers. We were told to go down the street to the "colored" cafeteria.

I was too young to understand what had just happened, but I will never forget the tears that ran down my mother's face, and the hurt that I saw in her eyes. That image burned a hole in my heart that will never, ever go away! These are just a couple examples of the long term residual effects of injustice.

Let's now turn our attention to the plight of the black American male athlete in the 60's, which consisted of the same mindset by white America, as it had for the black military men portrayed as inferior mentally. I remember when all American black quarterbacks coming out of college in the 60's and 70's, like Doug Williams, and Warren Moon (now in the Hall of Fame) were told that they were not good enough or intelligent enough for the NFL. They had to prove themselves by playing in the CFL (Canadian football league) or the AFL (American football league).

As is always the case, history has proven that this was not true, as both of these quarterbacks not only proved to be successful, but became hall of fame material as well. This sent a clear message to the black Americans that enough was not enough!

Compounding this situation was the fact that blacks had no role models at this time to look up to except war heroes and athletes. This tended to reinforce the notion that there were indeed two standards of criteria in which to judge blacks and whites. The resultant effect was a built in awareness and distrust in American values and the sense of equality.

Not only did this have a negative impact upon trust levels, but led to anger and frustration as well as disillusionment. When a person is angry, frustrated and disillusioned, the seedbeds for rebellion and disobedience are sowed! In light of these many abuses. An underlying distrust developed among blacks, and unfortunately caught up in the mix was the importance of education.

Time and cultural changes have affected the impact of this problem today, than it did when it appeared initially, but the residual effects are felt today. This is how the mindset of black America concerning the value of an education has been affected, and has henceforth produced this uneasy tension. The million dollar question is "how is trust restored?"

Roots in Slavery

The reason that this problem can be traced to slavery is because it was at this time, that the **myth** of blacks as somehow being a sub-human species was born as a mechanism to justify slavery's existence. One of the greatest gifts that God has given to mankind is the ability to reason, and this is the gift that we have abused more among all others.

We are masters at rationalizing away our sins and shortcomings under the guise of intelligence. Today, there is a movement on behalf of some government officials to change the constitutional safeguards of the past, which protected and ensured the rights of all people, especially black Americans to have the right to vote for one example.

Fifty years or so, this was not the law, thus leading to the **right to vote act.** This is being challenged today by those who attempt to say that this violates the civil rights of people, because the society has changed, and that this law is no longer necessary.

Who determines that these fifty years is long enough to overturn this legislation, when racism and discrimination still exist, even though we now refer to the word **nigger** as the "N" word! The mere reference to this is a clear indication that it is still too early to change these kinds of laws. The question to be asked is why is this subject an issue now? It is obvious then that the residual effects of racism still remain in the minds of people today.

At the time of this writing in 2014, there exists today a heated controversy about whether or not there is a need to have the "N" word eliminated entirely in TV commentaries, sporting events, locker rooms, schools, etc. The pervasive issues are that attempts to legislate these kinds of actions are ambivalent and controversial to say the least, thus inconclusive. While acceptable by some it is not acceptable by others including some blacks.

For example, the use of the word nigger by blacks, carry a significantly different meaning than when it is used by whites. Many blacks like me and others of my era, grew up using this word among ourselves as a matter of speech, with no derogatory meaning, yet conversely, if used by whites it was an insult. Hip- hop music today is saturated with the use of this word, and by and large it is accepted by many blacks.

As an example, if a black is interviewed and uses the term, a white commentator using it would be fired. If it is wrong for the commentator to use it, it should likewise be wrong for the black being interviewed as well! Right is right, and wrong is wrong regardless of who uses it.

The answer I believe is not the elimination of using the word, but in the meaning of it to the individual involved. I refrain from using it publically in conversation, because I realize that it is repugnant and offensive to many other blacks even to those of my era as well as those of today!

Arguments like this tend to test the limits of one's intelligence and memory, as time does succeed to a degree in dulling the effects of some events, especially to persons who have had **no firsthand** knowledge or experience with them. Conversely, time also reduces the awareness of the necessity to use racial slurs in the first place.

When you mentioned the racial events that took place in the 60' and 70's to young people today, they are horrified, and many can't believe that such things actually happened!

In 2013 here in Norfolk, VA, at Halloween, an attempt by a local community to get the county court to recognize a signed petition (later made public) to keep ethnic groups (blacks) from Trick or Treating in their neighborhood. Initially the argument began with a concern about over aged teens, but eventually degenerated into a racist tirade filled with slurs including the "N" word, specifically directed at blacks in general, including children who were referred to as little N's!

The letter which later aired over local news stations was roundly rejected by the viewers and the public as unbelievable. As repugnant as this is today for young people, especially young blacks who complain about the existing evils in today's society, older black parents such as myself can tell you, that such things used to be commonplace with no repercussions!

The Myth of inferiority

The problem with myths is that over time they grow into legends, and often it is very difficult to separate fact from fiction. All accounts of tales, experiences and folklore, all seem to grow with time, like the fisherman who catches a 2 pound fish. Five years later, the fish weighed 6 pounds! Therefore, one of the contributing factors in this dilemma is the passage of time in which this myth was able to persist.

This myth itself is a carryover from the days of slavery when then slaves (blacks of course) who were described as a type of sub-human species and therefore inferior, not being a complete person like whites were. It is hard to believe that something this illogical and irrational could ever have existed as believable. This myth of inferiority has persisted over time, even unto today.

If you tell a child as a single mother for instance, that he is a failure, and will be just like his no-good father, and will never amount to anything, you will produce a child who will be exactly that – a failure! As an example, in my own life as a high school senior, I was told by my counselor that I was not college material because of my struggles with grades.

Because I believed what she said, I did not attempt to go to college until I was thirty three years old. I now have three college degrees, one with honors in Philosophy! My point is that the residual effects of things that you are told can linger for many years.

In like fashion, this myth has taken its toll on the black psyche. I have no doubt that the persons who perpetrated this myth, and those who rejected it years ago, had no idea of the residual effects. Education somehow seems to have been the innocent bystander that became trapped in this warfare. It is now perceived in the black community with tongue in cheek, and as a result has become a strange bedfellow.

The unfortunate thing in this whole racial situation is that education was never a real factor in it. Education had nothing to do with the lynching of blacks by the KKK, or the burning of crosses on the lawns of black citizens. It had nothing to do with the segregation of the school system, or segregated eating facilities and public toilets. It had nothing to do with not allowing blacks to vote and to ride on integrated public busses, as well as having their churches bombed and set fire to.

Education had nothing to do with separate public drinking facilities and restrooms. It was innocent of being involved with housing discrimination and real estate steering policies, which perpetuated segregated communities. It had no role in the discriminatory hiring practices in the work place, with the lower classes of jobs designed for blacks, such as custodians, kitchen help, etc. It was not a part of the flawed judicial system that had a separate set of justice in the courts for black and whites.

Yet in spite of all this, education has suffered as a result, now being categorized along racial lines as being black or white. Any intelligent person should be able to clearly see this, but when racism clouds our thinking, everything else becomes secondary. You don't see the forest for the trees in the way. If you wear rose colored glasses, everything you see is rose colored!

Blacks need to realize that our own prejudices helped to contribute to the perpetuation of this dilemma! When we refer to education as somehow "whitewashing" us, we are hiding our own inferiorities and shortcomings under the umbrella of racism, while using it as a scapegoat to avoid our own apathy and lack of taking charge of our own destiny. We are helping to perpetuate this myth whether we want to admit it or not.

The challenge of older and experienced blacks is to educate our youth to this problem, and give them an understanding as to why this situation exists as it does, and their role in helping to eliminate it. You can't fight a war without knowing the enemy! Today's generation has inherited a problem that they don't fully understand, therefore, are unable to resolve it or even realize that they are helping to make this problem persist.

It is now time for us to stop allowing education to be trapped in this prison, while inhibiting the progress of the black community from flourishing! Here is where the black family, intellectuals, along with other older black individuals is needed to come together. It is vitally important as well, for whites to join the battle in doing away with the problem, being the principal culprits in this unfortunate situation to begin with. As long as we do nothing to change this dilemma, it will always continue to be a problem.

It is not just a black or white issue, but an American problem which has been allowed to become systemic, because of its long existence, and is now a black eye in our society for even letting it exist this long with nothing being done about it. If there are people who have been unaware of this situation prior to reading this manuscript, ignorance can no longer be used as an excuse, and that is precisely the reason for this writing.

CHAPTER TWO

The Perpetuation of the crisis

The culprit in this dilemma is racism and discrimination. These are the reasons that the myth was allowed to persist for so many years. Racial hatred and prejudice based on the color of a person, has now become an institutionalized subculture, often hidden behind laws and politics. The dynamic remained the same, it just **changed colors**! It is amazing how man can rationalize away his guilt in order to maintain that which he refuses to let go of whether right or wrong!

For example, years ago in North Carolina it became a **law** that made it illegal for whites and blacks to marry based on the biblical proof texting that God made us different for that reason (to remain separated). This law was recently stricken from the books, but look at how long it took for this to happen.

Once the practice of legalizing hidden racism as law, it opens up Pandora's Box for anything else to follow. For example, since federal legislation has outlawed restricting blacks from voting, a new movement is underfoot by various states to undermine the ability of thousands of poor, indigenous blacks from voter registration. This works by suppressing the poor who either do not have the means to obtain valid ID, which often includes a driver's license, proof of residency (often recent bills mailed to the person's legal place of residence in their name), valid state ID, etc.

The **Daily Advance**, the official newspaper of Elizabeth City, North Carolina, on August 26, 2013, on page 4A states: "I don't think it would be an exaggeration to say that there is a lot of characterization of North Carolina's new voting laws as drastic, Jim Crow-like, shocking, and extreme, etc." In like fashion, the ECSU (Elizabeth City State University) which is predominately black was recently embroiled in controversy over a voting rights issue involving a black graduate student who sought to run for City Council.

The Pasquotank County Board of election ruled that because he was not a "permanent" resident, he was ineligible to run for office, and the students could not vote because of the same restriction. It was appealed to the North Carolina Board of elections which ruled in favor of the student's right to run for office, and also allowing the students the right to vote in September 2013, stating that the word "permanent" should mean that students can reside at a place 365 days a year."

These three cases cited above only serve to illustrate what can happen when states are allowed to form their own laws, originally called "state's rights."

I could list numerous examples of how this same practice has been used over the years, to blur the difference between morality, ethics, right and wrong as they pertain to moral issues, but that is not the purpose of this writing. Now that the color of the argument has shifted, the stage is now set for the **same** issue to become one of a social matter rather a moral one.

Changing the color of the problem does not change the nature of it. A spade is still a spade regardless. We will maintain our focus exclusively on the issue of education, thus keeping the main thing the main thing! **Expediency** is often the norm in human rationalization, and morality just gets in the way, or slows what is termed as progress!

Now that the issue of racism has become a legal and social one, rather than a moral one, it can now be handled as such by hiding behind the façade of just another problem to deal with. This method is a clever way in which to mask the guilt of the past, and now create a new way of dealing with an old issue as simply a mistake. However, perception is not always reality. Let's look at the way in which this deception was done.

The focus is now shifted away from the black and white issue, to one of the **legal** separation of the races, including those along educational lines such as separate but equal. Once this is done, it now becomes the ground swell for the **Jim Crow law** of so-called separate, but equal education, done within the framework of school Segregation. Remember, as irrational and absurd as this may sound, at one time segregation was a **legal** option in which to maintain discrimination!

Jim Crow law and education

Social matters are more easily handled than moral ones, simply because now that they are legal, as long as you don't break the law you've committed no wrong. The problem with this type of reasoning is that it is illogical, because the **major premise** of the argument is flawed, in that it is OK to have a separate society, even though our constitution says otherwise; that all men are created equal, with certain God given rights of freedom, liberty and the pursuit of happiness.

In the philosophy of logic, if the major or minor premises are flawed, then the conclusion must also be flawed. It is impossible to get a logical conclusion from an illogical argument. The problem with this particular line of thinking here is that if the premise is accepted as valid, simply because it's legal, then the conclusion is also accepted as valid.

This is what happened when the majority of Americans accepted this practice, and why Jim Crow laws lasted for so long until the myth of separate but equal education became exposed. This educational system was never equal! White students attended schools in nice neighborhoods, with the best trained and qualified teachers, nice facilities, and less crowded classrooms, while black students were crammed together in poor inner city neighborhoods, with overcrowded classrooms, fewer teachers, often not the best trained and qualified, and often in run down facilities.

The problem here is that the **subliminal** message sent to blacks was that while education may be important, it is not determining. By not being determining, we simply mean that it is merely the means to an end. The end is in achieving the American dream that an education is the key to success, but the subtle message sent here is in stark contrast to what America has portrayed from the beginning.

There is no denying that this inconsistency is what has contributed to the mixed message sent to the black community concerning education. However, what is done in darkness, will soon come to the light. There is always a price to be paid for every decision that we make as humans. This is no exception! The price in this case is the creation of a dilemma that has prompted the writing of this book for both blacks and whites.

There is always a reason why distrust develops among people. When it comes to education, blacks have felt that they have been sold a bill of goods! The former **Jim Crow** law is the shining example of this type of hypocrisy that underlies this particular issue. Racism and discrimination was attempted to be covered up and pretended as if that they never existed. Mankind is a master of masking his guilt by manufacturing deceptions to cover up his mistakes! These laws are shining examples of this practice.

This is the reason why this nation was literally **torn apart** when President Linden B. Johnson signed into law the desegregation of public schools, and the institution of **bussing** to achieve racial balance in education thus exposing this hypocrisy!. Riots broke out all over the nation as evidence that too many white citizens had believed this ideology. What is amazing is that there were blacks who disagreed with bussing as well!

I lived through this turmoil and experienced the climate of the time firsthand, but to this day I still cannot understand why some blacks were opposed to this law. I could understand why many whites were opposed to it, because this was stripping away some of their powers, but at this time blacks had no power! I later discovered that many whites were opposed to the Jim Crow law of separate but equal education, but did not speak out and therefore became known as the **silent majority.**

This inner division among blacks during the racial riots of the 60's, only points out too clearly that blacks were divided over most of the issues of the civil rights movement. This division even permeated into some of the black churches!

In Columbus, Ohio where I grew up, there were churches that would not allow Dr. King to use their facilities as a platform to speak, or to organize and plan strategies for upcoming events. Because this kind of news makes the newspapers, many whites were now made aware of the inner turmoil within the black the community itself.

This division over the civil rights movement, unfortunately, affected the educational process as well, which led to the notion by some black militants and radicals, as being a tool to indoctrinate and assimilate blacks into white society, thus creating the term of being "whitewashed" by higher education. This ludicrous and ridiculous mindset, however, still remains in the minds of some black folk even today.

I have always maintained that one of our biggest obstacles as black Americans is our inability to stick together in the face of adversity. In the 60's and 70's during the civil rights era, I could understand the work of Malcolm X, alongside of Martin Luther King, JR., as both sides complimenting the other, but some blacks still remained opposed to Martin Luther King.

I could understand white opposition to his non-violent approach to social change, because it brought shame to bear on their violent actions perpetrated against defenseless black men, women and children, but to be divided as a black culture about the works of the non-violent approach of Dr. King is still a mystery to me. I hope that this division was over the tactic or the approach of non-violence as a tool, and not over the ideology or concept of the civil rights struggle itself.

People in general, black or white, are always divided over political issues such as party affiliation and tactics, as the battle over Women's Rights in society demonstrated. The works of Dr. King, however, was not just about justice and equality in the political and social arenas for black folk, but justice for all people and races, whites included. It was designed to raise the **moral** consciousness of America over racial and gender inequities!

The perception of education today

When you look at the **landscape** of education today, it's no wonder that young people today cannot believe the way things were, just as recently as the times of their own parents. I have a hard time even today, convincing young people of the tremendous progress that has been made in education from the time of my own childhood until now.

This is part of my own frustration and anxiety. Young people today have not lived through this terrible time in our history, and are not impacted by it as the previous generation was, who had to literally give their lives for the right to vote and to receive a college education. They are apt to relegate these people to the status of irrelevancy, as they often do their parents, which of course I know we can all relate to!

I remember vividly the time that the National Guard had to be called into Little Rock Arkansas to Central high school in the sixties, to allow seven black teenage students to attend high school there. When you try to relate this experience to the youth of today, it is received tongue-in-cheek, or in a ho-hum fashion.

Now when you look at the sports being playing today in our universities, the majority of the players are black in football, basketball, and track and field. I remember the time when running back Prentice Gault in the 70's, was the first black in the history of the University of Oklahoma allowed to compete in football! Now look at the program! Yet, in spite of all the changes that have been made, the damage had already been done. The psyche of the black community has been damaged as it pertained to education because of this. This has led to what I term as the **black hybrid intellectual.**

My interpretation of this kind of hybrid individual is referred to in the book "**Too black for white and too white for black**" by Dr. James Earls 2012. I have chosen, however, to refer to his writing which only focused on the race issue, to exclusively focus on the issue of higher education in the black community in this writing.

Dr. Earls is correct in his assessment, however, about the plight of the black man in America. With all of the changes that have taken place in the nation in the past fifty years or so, the black man is much more accepted in the mainstream of society today, but still with many reservations.

America has recently owned up to its sins of the past as it relates to racial and social injustices of blacks and other minorities. Slavery has been acknowledged as a black eye for America, and the treatment of Native Americans (Indians) has been acknowledged as well. This progress has not come about, unfortunately, without white backlash and reservations which we will discuss in detail later.

Like the old saying goes, "you can take the person out of the ghetto, but you can't take the ghetto out of the person." Many whites today still yearn for the return of yesteryear when whites were the majority of the population, and more or less had their way in the social and economic arenas. Concessions were often made out of necessity, especially with the advent of the civil rights movement of the 60's.

The problem is that prejudice and racial hatred are in the minds of people, and no amount of legislation or changes in the law can erase them! This involves a host of numerous complicated issues that lie outside of the premise of this writing. This is precisely why I chose to limit this conversation to the area of education, particularly as it concerns the nature of higher education (college) in the black community.

Ask almost any black college graduate about how he feels in his own community, and they will tell you that it not very comfortable! What a shame and a waste, but it is not without a reason.

CHAPTER THREE

The result of the crisis: The hybrid black intellectual

The juxtaposition of the black male intellectual and his acceptance or non-acceptance within his own community as we have discussed earlier, has led him to become a **hybrid** being. His plight is one of Self Understanding..."who am I?" He has become a social misfit, no longer seen by many blacks as an authentic black person, in the true sense of the word among his peers.

This is a very awkward situation and is completely unsettling psychologically. Here you are with your own people, sharing their experiences, or trying to, looking like everyone else, going to the same stores and walking the same streets, having the same neighbors, your children going to the same schools etc., yet feeling like an outsider and unwanted by many in the community.

It leaves him to wonder what he did wrong other than getting an education, which we were always told you should do if possible. He still feels and looks as black as he always has, and feel no differently except in the way he we talks, and the way that he now views the things he sees around him.

This is the way that life should evolve every day. Nothing remains the same in life and this change should reflect our growth as individuals. This feeling of isolation is something that one must feel and experience as an individual, and which cannot always be articulated until it's experienced. How do you cope with feeling like an outsider with your own people?

I believe that most black Americans do not understand this situation, and many are unaware that it even exists except the individual involved. I feel that a certain amount of resentment on the behalf of those who treat this person differently now, is because of their growth and the lack of their own. It is a sign of jealousy.

This is precisely what the issue is in this dilemma! This individual has changed on the **inside** but, unfortunately, people look on the **outside** and judge accordingly. In spite of internal changes, one is expected to still act and relate externally as they always have. This begs the question of am I accepted as **what** I am, or **who** I am?

At the same time, this individual does not fit the mold of the white community as well. So the question is, how is he to understand himself now that he doesn't seem to fit anywhere in society, and has become a social misfit? Being a social misfit, however, is nothing more than a state of mind.

Have you ever experienced the feeling of being alone in a crowded room or gathering? Even if some of the faces are familiar and you know the surrounding, it still does not ease the feeling. It's as if you are being tolerated, but not really being accepted or appreciated. One could make the argument that this individual is inwardly insecure, and lacks the things which will allow him to be comfortable as he is.

One evidence of a maturing adult is the ability of establish their own individuality. This is accomplished in part when we are able to focus on our own agenda as **primary,** in spite of the differing agendas around us. It is not the responsibility of outside influences to determine our place in the world, rather our responsibility to fit where we choose to fit, and then to maintain the direction that we need to travel for ourselves.

This is called **intestinal fortitude** and an unwavering sense of resolve and determination. Without these values, it is impossible to become what you want to become, and to make the necessary changes that you deem necessary. In life, it is not critical where you are, but where you are going!

This is the lesson that young folk today need to learn and understand. If the dream of Martin Luther King is ever to be realized in this society, it must be done by advancing the gains that have been accomplished since the 60's and 70's, without lamenting continually about what has not been accomplished. Looking back only limits one's ability to move forward. This is precisely where the teaching of older adults to the young, need to take place.

Because of this loss of belief in himself, and who and what he is, in spite of the opinions of those around him, he is apt to give in to peer- pressure in order to avoid being different. I believe that this is what drives many of our young men today to affiliate with gangs and the sub culture they represent.

In its true sense, when blacks are made to feel this way about themselves, it is a clear example of how we are still enslaved in the worst prison in the world, that of the mind! This is a clear indication of a type of a Paranoid mindset, and a sense of immaturity among blacks today as a whole. In our lethargy, it appears as though we are waiting for another savior like Martin Luther King, to come and lead us to the Promised Land.

Blacks today need to realize that the prisons that enslaved us in the past are gone! We can only enslave and limit ourselves by the scope and freedom of our own minds. The Bible tells us that a people perish without a dream or vision. That is precisely what black Americans need to do – rediscover what it is to dream. Dr. King's leadership was based on his **dream!**

The result of this of this type of Cultural Apathy is the creation of a dichotomy pertaining to the role of education in the life of the black Americans, who have now become isolated, with education now a strange bedfellow. This is not only a shame, but a tragedy! For decades black Americans have received mixed signals and insincere rhetoric told to them by whites, about the value of education to them.

These false subliminal messages sent to black Americans about the value of education has had a lasting effect, but part of the blame must be shouldered by the black community for not rejecting them as false. There comes a time when individuals must think for themselves as adults, and not be manipulated by what others tell them.

In essence, what this says about the maturity level as a whole of black society is that we are still in an **adolescent** mindset instead of an adult one. The Apostle Paul says in 1 Corinthians 11: "When I was child I thought as a child, but when I became a man, I put away childish things."

Many blacks are not going to accept this assessment as it pertains to them today as a whole, and will be prone to calling it a whitewashed or Uncle Tom version! Be that as it may, I think that it is a valid criticism of the immature way in which we think, and the existing apathy and feeling of powerlessness that we feel.

This is not to say that all white Americans were a part and parcel of this deception originally. Proponents of the college **quota system** for example, now seemingly defunct, was an example of the movement designed to ensure that a fair percentage of blacks were allowed to enroll in college, even with some academic deficiencies, caused by the so-called Jim Crow laws of equal but separate schools discussed earlier.

The aforementioned assessments here, only point to the fact that every white man is not your enemy, and every black man is not your brother. Many whites saw the need at that time for federal legislation to ensure the rights of the poor, indigenous and black citizens of America.

A word of caution needs to be mentioned here for those persons who feel that we have come far enough in race relations, that we can now begin to eliminate some of these laws, such as a recent attempt to do away with school bussing, the voting right act of the sixties, and the aforementioned quota system, simply because some people feel that the "time is right." to repeal them. For those people who do not learn from the past they are doomed to repeat it! Let's not turn back the clock America!

If you can imagine for a moment as blacks have, the torment of having put aside many of the so-called pleasures of life, in order to accomplish a life-long dream for yourself **and** your family, only to discover that your accomplishment is scorned by the very persons that you seek affirmation from; as well as the society which encouraged it and then denied it's impact, can have devastating effects on the individual involved.

In this state of mind, one not only feels isolated, but betrayed, made a mockery of, feeling foolish to an extent, disillusioned, and bitter! It must be analogous to a man without a country! This is the **plight** of the black intellectual. Even though we now have a black president in the white house, he is the **exception** to the rule, and we should not be misled! Many Americans voted for Obama because they doubted his nationality and race initially. He was not the typical black from the hood!

Every now and then, **accepted** blacks like golfer Tiger Woods, entertainer and humanitarian Bill Cosby, retired General Colin Powell and Supreme Court Judge Clarence Thomas, escape and defy the odds, but with rare exception. This only helps feed the **illusion** that you can go as far as you want to go if you are willing to pay the price. This illusion in my opinion is primarily responsible for the creation of the hybrid black intellectual.

The resultant effect is the juxtaposition of education and its role in the black experience. Because of this ambivalence, "blackness" and education have become strange bedfellows (sharing the same bed, but with no intimacy). As stated earlier, the genesis of this problem can be traced to the historical impact of the myth of black inferiority!

CHAPTER FOUR

The hybrid intellectual in the black community

Perceived Whitewashing

First of all there is no such thing as a white wash in education. It is utter nonsense when you hear that a black man going off to college, is going away to become whitewashed by the white man's educational system! Education, first of all **does not** have a color, only a perception. How can I become whitewashed without losing my skin color?

We will discuss this later in detail. However, when one is separated from his environment for a spell, it can **color** the way he **thinks** by allowing the individual to see his surroundings in a much different way than he did when he was in the midst of it.

This is much like the dynamic experienced when one quits smoking. The insanity of the addiction to smoking becomes painfully clear when he discovers that the very first thing he does in the morning is to reach for a cigarette, even before his feet hit the floor. His time spent after smoking one cigarette, is to count the time before his next one, thus surviving from one smoke to the next, much like the alcoholic who lives from one drink to the next.

If that is not enough, he remembers the time that he had one cigarette in his mouth, one lit in the ashtray, and another that he was smoking but couldn't find. Then he remembers the panic of running out of cigarettes and money at the same time, and groveling through the ashtray in the car, looking for a butt to make a roach to feed his addiction (ex-smokers know exactly what I'm talking about).

One of the problems here is that the addicted person does not see his plight, because he is in the **midst** of it and has become a part. The smoker becomes immune to its effects in time. When he smokes, he does not smell the smoke on those who do, but once he quits he notices no smell on those who don't. It's amazing how that works. The insanity that accompanies addiction is often that it cannot be seen, because it becomes a way of life to the addict. One simply buys into it as normal!

One of the principles that a recovering addict must live by, is changing the environment that he is used to in order to get a new start. Only then can he see the effects of his addiction on his behavior. In analogous fashion, the same principle applies to the Black American who goes away to college to receive his education.

Being black never changes, but the **way** in which he thinks should always change, or it should. If one continues to think the same way as he grows, this means that he has ceased to learn. We should learn something new every day, otherwise we stop living and begin to only exist. How can one get older without changing? Does a fifteen year old still think the same way he did when he was six?

Of course education expands the horizon of one's world… it should! As our world expands while learning, it changes the way that we see things. Once this happens, it is impossible to see things exactly as we did before. Herein is the threat to the black intellectual.

The perceived threat to blackness

Once being temporarily separated from his former environment, and learning new and different ways of thinking and life skills, the intellectual can now look back on his former way of life, and become a **critic** in a positive way, much like the recovering addict can look back on the causes and triggers of his former addition. The black intellectual now becomes painfully aware of the negative and the Counter Productive behaviors of his people and their former way of life.

One thing that he recognizes immediately is the departure of blacks from the real strength of their culture which is religion. The black intellectual now sees that blacks have fallen away from the church, which has always been the backbone of its culture and resiliency! From the roots of slavery, the black community has always maintained an unwavering sense of strength and morality from the church, which has always been the social and moral standard bearer of its essence. In my opinion, this is where the sense of the loss of blackness **begins!**

We are currently feeling a loss of power and strength because of this, and have mistakenly referred to it as a loss of blackness! All that we know is that this is a loss of something which must be labeled because American society is experiencing a falling away from the church in this so-called age of enlightened and post resurrection mentality. Blacks have failed to realize that they too have also joined this mainstream of declining religiosity, thus a perceived loss of so called blackness!

The key operative word here is **perceived!** Perception is not reality, but since so many individuals are prone to believe what they **think** they see, they form their opinions accordingly. Ironically, the problem is that sense the term "blackness" is exactly that, only a term, formed by individual subjective interpretation, the concept therefore is an **illusion**! Since it is not a concrete reality which lacks a specific definition as discussed earlier, the perceived so-called threat is likewise an illusion.

How can you threaten something that does not exist in actuality? The threat therefore, only exists in the mind and imagination of the person in which it is imagined. Therefore, it must be surmised that education is in no way a threat to the existence of blackness!

The fallacy of the threat

In my opinion, the only persons that feel threatened by higher education like college are the ones who do not have one, or have very little, and do not know the full value of it. In like fashion, the people who love money are by and large the people who do not have much of it. Just ask those who have more money than they can spend in a life time, how they feel about it. For those individuals who feel that education is a threat of some sort, tell me how? What does it threaten? Certainly not blackness, we've established that!

A threat is the **anticipation** of an adverse event that **could possibly** take place! Often people can feel threatened by an imaginary adversary. When this occurs and causes the individual to become unable to function normally, it is diagnosed as a form of **Paranoia**. Is it possible that some blacks using higher education as the scapegoat for feeling a measure of insecurity as a race, be a form of this disease? Let's examine this possibility and arrive at our own conclusion.

A critique of blackness

The question that begs to be answered is does blackness exist at all, and if it does what is it all about? People coin phrases all the time that often have no meaning at all. For instance, the term" nerd," (for an individual who is different}, "sweet" (that has nothing to do with taste at all); "cool" (that has nothing to do with temperature), etc. The list goes on indefinitely. I know these are slang expressions of what is considered "hip" talk (which by the way has nothing to do with a body part.)

When you say that a person is black, and it doesn't refer to skin color, then what is it? Does it not fall into the same category as the words listed above? If the color of my skin is black by birth, how then can I lose it without dying or suffering from the disease of vitiligo (the loss of skin color in blacks)? You hear the expression used frequently that so and so is not "black enough." How can this be? Does it mean that a dark skinned brother is blacker than a light skinned one? This is the only thing that makes any sense in this nonsensical statement!

When we make a statement of any kind, shouldn't it be a logical one that makes common sense? Therefore, I find it difficult to understand how getting a college education affects my skin color. If it doesn't, then what does it affect and what does it threaten?

Does being "black" threaten the sloppy way that some of us dress or walk wide legged while holding up our pants, because we don't wear belts or even if we wear them?... It should. Here is what I don't understand. Why wear a belt if it does not hold up your pants? What purpose is it then serving? Why would you walk uncomfortably holding up your pants, when that's what a belt is designed to do?

They put sizes on clothes so that people can buy them and look nice. What purpose does it serve to buy clothes two and three sizes too big? What is the purpose of exposing one's **underwear** as outwear as many men do? Can you imagine how a woman would look if she walked around showing off half of her thong above her pants? What kind of message would she be sending about herself? Under pants are designed to be worn **under** pants. That's just common sense!

The question that begs to be answered here is what does the purpose of sloppy and indecent dress serve other than making an anti-social statement? If it is done to mimic the dress of gangsters and criminals as it seems to do, of what good purpose does it serve mankind and society to glorify that which is undesirable? Imitation is said to be the highest form of flattery. Is this the best statement that we as black Americans can make about ourselves?

Does it threaten the vulgar and disrespectful language that some blacks use, when it comes to our back women? ...It should. If a white person would refer to a black woman as a Hoe or the B word, it would instantly be fighting words to blacks, because it would imply disrespect, the same way as whites using the N word would be!

Yet too much of the lyrics used in black rap videos and CD's use this type of language describing black women as Hoes, and black men as "N's", blasting loudly on car radios on public streets. Does being black mean, it is OK for blacks to disrespect black women in this manner but whites cannot? If it's wrong for them it ought to be equally as wrong for blacks. **Wrong is wrong and right is right** and the two know no color! It is inexcusable, period! Being black does not give us the right to disrespect each other, and it is not **cute!**

Does being "black" mean accepting or making excuses for the way that we murder and kill each other, often in our own neighborhoods?... It should not! What troubles me is that too many blacks have a tendency of accepting this as a way of life in the ghetto or the "hood."

The truth about these types of crimes is just another example of black paranoia. These crimes of murder, robbery and killings by blacks, do not take place normally in white neighborhoods, primarily because the police will investigate any murder in a white neighborhood committed by a black, much more aggressively than one committed in a black neighborhood.

Black criminals know this and so they commit their crimes in a safer environment – the black community. Here is what is disturbing. Can't we see what this is doing to us as a people? When you look at the numbers of blacks who kill other blacks, and the ridiculous rate of the incarceration of our young black males due to drugs and other crimes, are we not practicing the **genocide** of ourselves?

No longer can the KKK or other white hate groups such as the Neo Nazis, be blamed for the genocide of black folk. If the truth be known, if I was a white man who wanted to see blacks disappear from the landscape of our society, I would just leave them alone, because they are now doing my job for me!

Does it threaten the way that some blacks often discourage other black students in college from devoting long hours to academic disciplines and study by accusing them of trying to be white? How is striving to become a better person be ridiculed? If this threatens the so-called notion of "blackness," It should.

As long as young black college students fail to realize that the purpose of getting a college degree is for their benefit, regardless of what others say who still harbor past resentments, there will always be the dilemma of higher education as a strange bedfellow in the black community, keeping us an enslaved people. It is now incumbent upon the young who have inherited this problem, along with the older generation who have lived with this problem, to overcome it together!

Does a college degree threaten being disrespectful to our mothers and parents, as well as other adults in authority? It should. Blacks, especially the black male, are notoriously known for being intolerant of remarks made about their mothers outside of playing the dozens by other blacks.

This primarily extends to the sensitivity of black men concerning their mothers because of the absence of fathers in their lives. In my own experience, I never knew my biological father because he left my mother when I was eight years old, the oldest of five children, to raise us by herself. This is all too common a story in black families.

Have you ever notice how black athletes always give a greeting to their mothers during an interview? This is why black males have such a high regard for their mothers. That's a tragedy because every child needs to have a mother and a father. That's how God has ordained families to be!

Does "blackness" threaten the respect of others, like the excessive loud music, with its abusive and often vulgar lyrics that blast from our vehicles? No! If one enjoys this type of music, keep it at a controlled level, because not everyone enjoys it. This type of behavior, I believe, is only an attempt to get attention, and can be determined as a sense of insecurity and low Self Esteem. Do you notice how they glance in your vehicle to see it you notice them?

Does a college education threaten the ghetto and "gangsta" way that we express ourselves in the hood, with slurred and lazy speech habits, often mispronouncing words, sometimes intentionally, and using incomplete sentences as an attempt to appear less academic? No! This can be understood as a form of anti- social behavior.

Does it threaten the way that some black males have a habit of grabbing their crotch excessively, especially while talking? It doesn't take a rocket scientist to understand that this is only mimicking gang behavior. What is disturbing about this, is if this is the role model that our young people are embracing, it should be a concern for all of us. The sad thing about all of this is that too many black parents today choose to turn their head the other way, instead of confronting their child about their conduct.

This is where young parents today miss the boat. In times past, black parents, especially mothers, would always confront their children about negative behavior, often in social venues! As children, we were often chastised in church, grocery stories, etc. CSB today, however has affected the way that parents can chastise or correct their children in public. As a black parent, I don't need someone from the white community telling me how to raise my black child!

Does being "black" threaten the way that we **allow** drugs and gangs to infest our communities and poison our children? No! You can use the rationale that blacks are not responsible for the presence of drugs in our communities, or for the pushers that sell them. Some use the excuse that the mob or white persons in authority allow these drugs to infiltrate our communities.

While there may be a grain of truth in this statement, it is no excuse for **our** behavior, because we are the ones responsible for putting this poison into our own bodies. No one forces us to do this, especially to our own children! You hear these persons claim that it is easy money, and if they don't do it, somebody else will. What kind of sense does that make?

Does it threaten our **security** as a race, because we expect the white man to change things for us instead of taking these matters into our own hands? No! The best person to change your life is **you**! Nobody but blacks can be responsible for the lack of intestinal fortitude and lethargy plaguing our people today, leading to a sense of resignation and powerlessness. I remember the words of my mother when I was a child; "The only way that someone can be better than you, is to be a better person."

Black on black attitudes

Let's now take an honest look at ourselves as black folk and the way in which we have historically treated each other. The current younger generation can be excused from this analysis, but even then they need to just be observant and pay attention to these traits. They will see that many of these problems **still** exist today, if they are not in a state of denial!

In our **supportive relationships** of one another, our lack of this is the source of jokes and pathetic illustrations such as the **crabs in the barrel** syndrome, which depicts blacks who keep other blacks from overcoming their current situations because of jealousy, envy and selfishness. This fable comes from black people about themselves and not from whites.

This illustration was highlighted in the black TV series the Redd Foxx show in the 70's **Sanford and Son, and preached by ministers over the years in many of our black churches. It** goes something like this: Blacks are depicted as being like crabs trapped in a barrel.

When one crab tries to climb up and out of the barrel, other crabs reach up and pull him back down! This is symbolic of the way that we fail to be supportive of one another. We do this in several ways. If you are a college student and you deride another black student for choosing to study faithfully after classes, in order to get the best grades they're capable of, rather than partying after hours and calling them book worms or nerds, then you are exhibiting this type of behavior!

If you ostracize or make a person feel an outsider just because they are different, then you participate in this "Crabs in the barrel Syndrome". "Blacks need to learn unity from other ethnic groups, such as the Jew, East Indian, etc., about how to stick together to accomplish a common goal. We as blacks lament about how foreigners come into our communities and take over our local businesses. There are reasons as to why this exists.

While it's true that many of these ethnic groups are given lines of credit that many blacks are denied in order to start their businesses, what they do with this opportunity is much different than what we as blacks do. They will support each other, and uplift those who struggle in their business endeavors by lending them assistance in any way they can in order to help them succeed.

Notice the buying habits of Orientals and Asians for example in purchasing automobiles. The vast majority will buy vehicles manufactured in Japan and European counties. This is how they participate in the economic wellbeing of their homelands even while living in America.

Black business practices

Pay particular attention to the poor public relation skills that we treat our black customers in everyday business transactions. How many times has a black Proprietor said to you as a customer with a smile, while making eye to eye contact "We appreciate your business and look forward to seeing you again?" A handshake is almost always nonexistent! Many times when you are searching for an item in a convenience store, and having trouble locating it, the service person at the counter seldom comes voluntarily to give assistance!

The importance of public relation skills are not practiced or even known by many black counter persons, like cashiers and other personnel. These skills are the very ones that make people return! Sometimes you leave a black establishment feeling as though they have done you a favor by waiting on you. It makes me wonder just how they are trained to do what they do. Even without being trained in PR skills, it's not difficult to practice common courtesy!

When we patronage black professionals for example, such as doctors or lawyers, etc., it is usually with an aura of distrust **and hesitancy.** We question their credentials, education, **and** qualifications. Conversely, often black professionals treat their black clients in a less professional way than they do their white customers. When we go to white professionals, this is seldom the case, because it is good business to make your customers feel important.

We are often treated by black professionals like second class citizens, or welfare persons, which come to them with their hands out! Many have poor bedside manners when it comes to their own, as opposed to the way that they treat their white clients. Many times, however, we expect our black professionals to treat us differently simply because we are black, by giving us much lower charges, extended time to pay our bills, even when we see signs posted that payment is expected when served.

We honor these notices in white establishments without hesitation or reluctance, because we understand that business is business, except when it comes to black businesses, where you often hear blacks say "come on brother, give a brother a break." These are further examples of the crabs in the barrel syndrome.

We often wonder why in our black community's foreign individuals come in and take over the small businesses, such as drug stores, gas stations, and food services and thrive. Often it is because we don't support our own local business entrepreneurs!

A case in point is a local food store owner in Columbus, Ohio in the 70's, that I remember who ran a thriving super market for years. He made one fatal mistake! One day he drove his new late model vehicle to work and parked it in his personal parking place. It was seen, naturally, by many black customers. It was not long afterwards that the conversation in the neighborhood was about how the owner of the store was getting rich on their dollars.

Needless to say it was not long afterwards that many blacks stopped patronizing his store, and went around the block to the white man's store that owned four new cars, and gave him their business without hesitation! This is a clear example of the "crabs in the barrel" syndrome, exhibiting distrust, jealousy and envy that we have with one another.

If you use or sell drugs in your community, and use the excuse that "if I don't do it, somebody else will," you are exhibiting the kind of behavior, which contributes to the demise of your own community and people. Using the excuse that you are not responsible for drugs being in your community, is no reason for you giving it to yourself or others to make easy money.

Using a gun just because it is easily attained and available, is no reason for using it to kill another individual regardless of color, and then claim that poverty or neighborhood conditions, including the proclivity of gangs are the culprits, then you are exhibiting this kind of behavior. As the old axiom goes, "guns don't kill people, people kill people."

If you support or participate in musical lyrics that demean and belittle our black women by using words such as the "B" word, Hoes", etc., showing them in videos shaking their booties like whores, while the men grab their crotches, are exhibiting this kind of behavior, because it degrades our culture as blacks. I remember not too long ago, when our music talked about "I'll always love you," "Forever mine," or "Treat her like a lady," were the hits of the day.

I'm not suggesting that we return to yesteryear, but just look at the **changes** in the nature of the music involved. They say that music usually tells the tale of the period in which it is found, much like the music of the 60's and 70's which depicted the civil uprisings of the day such as "give peace a chance," the search for a positive black identity such as "I'm black and I'm proud," etc., are a couple of examples of this.

My question today is what does our music today reflect? What does it say about us as a people and as a race? When white society sees our videos and listen to our music, what images do we portray about ourselves?

In conclusion, if all of the things mentioned above are true, how is **blackness** threatened by changing these undesirable behaviors? These are not issues of blackness, but of conduct. Regardless of my behavior as a person, nothing can change who and what I am but me! Regardless of what anyone thinks about me as a person, **I will always be black**. I have no other choice. I was born this way, thanks to the Lord!

Criticism is seldom received gracefully, even if it is **constructive**, and is intended to uplift, rather than tear down. This is my intent for writing this critique, because I love my black brother and sisters, and I am extremely proud to be black, by whatever name you want to call me. Nobody on the face of this earth, red, yellow, black or white can change who and what I am, only God, because he made me to be what he intended me to be. That's why there is not another me in the whole of creation.

This type of critique by a black of blacks, will fail to endear me with many persons in the inner city. Some examples of this is evidenced when looking at the way such blacks as Bill Cosby, black preachers, schoolteachers, and other black professionals who speak out about these issues. They are often seen as being a part of the establishment, rather than as advocate for constructive change!

Man is a **gregarious** creature meaning that he is a communal being who needs to be connected to other humans. This is what created the saying that "no man is an island." This need to be connected to others has both positive and negative consequences. Because we are all different in temperament and personality, we have a tendency to feel more comfortable, and secure with those that we identify with.

O.J. Brown in his book "Christianity and the class struggle" refers to these positive and negative consequences as those things that tend to build a a community around these likes and dislikes, but which often end up, however, excluding those who do not share this common bond. We see evidences of this in churches on Sundays, which is probably the most segregated time in our nation, which is an oxymoron.

An attempt to try and understand this dichotomy is often referred to as the H**omogeneous Principle** of worship, which in itself is not racism, but one of comfort and identity. It is undeniable that the style of preaching, worship, music, and fellowship, play key roles in our worship experience. Because of these gregarious gatherings, others that do not belong in our "**group**" are often stigmatized and ostracized!

As an example of this, is when I worked as a full time staff chaplain at a major hospital in Toledo, Ohio during the 90's, as the only black administrator on a staff of over one hundred professionals. Often when it came to handling a crisis which involved a black family or individuals, I was always summoned to "put out the fire."

This seemed to happen frequently in the emergency room where people sometime wear their emotions on their sleeves, and are sometimes unpredictable. In other situations dealing with ethical and medical consults concerning matters of life and death, some black families involved would periodically label me as "**one of them**"(the establishment) simply by association.

Because of this, undoubtedly some blacks would label me as an "uncle tom" because I was perceived as breaking this common bond mentioned above by Harold Brown. This points to how susceptible we are as blacks to segregate ourselves.

The myth of the intellectual's loss of blackness

Because of what the black intellectual is and what he represents, is one of the things which fuel this argument, because he is not seen as a part of the gregarious group mentioned above, by virtue of his education. He is perceived as being "whitewashed" with diminishing blackness, because he is seen as thinking white. The question which intrigues me is since when is thinking right thinking white?

There is no difference with this myth than the one of Jim Crow law. Both are based on a fallacy of thought, but like the Jim Crow laws which survived so long, they thrive on longevity and eventual acceptance. This fallacy and myth of diminishing blackness, however, falls prey to the same demise. They only last for a season, until their practice of disguising racism in this case, or legality in the former, is exposed as a sham.

There is no denying that linking higher education with a loss of blackness is a disguise for rejecting education, much like the Jim Crow laws of the past were a disguise for racial hatred, the real culprit of this line of thinking is an absurd and twisted mindset.

Once higher education is allowed to become a white and black issue similar to the Jim Crow patterns of thinking, is easier to sell its discriminatory ideology to a vulnerable mindset. One form is no better than the other! Because this way of thinking hides behind the mask of racism and prejudice regardless of where it comes from (a black perspective this time), it must out of necessity be rejected as well. It is ludicrous to allow education to become the scapegoat of a racist mentality of being "whitewashed."

CHAPTER FIVE

The hybrid intellectual in the white community

Now we come to the part of this dilemma where the rubber hits the road. This is where those blacks who espouse the issue of losing blackness may feel a measure of vindication, and the white community must share a part of this blame. Every rumor or myth always has a basis in fact to a smaller or larger degree. Here whites are a victim of their own deceitfulness and past sins of discrimination, half- truths, and deceptions. Here, the white community is tripping over its own feet because the past sooner or later always catches up to us.

As stated earlier in this presentation, the residual effects of slavery, the perpetuation of lies such as black inferiority, hiding behind the factitiousness of unjust laws, have all served to feed this crisis which now plagues us as a society. When we abuse history as we have done over the past decades, history has its own way of deceiving us as a result.

For example, there is a sense that the future is already with us as reflected in the nature of today's religious thought, as being a **post resurrection society.** The mindset today as already having the future present with us, is reflected in the way that many churches approach religion today, as having already received the coming of the kingdom. Sermons by and large are all about **receiving** the blessings of the lord promised to us if we just ask for them and little else.

Somehow if we just do the right thing like sending "seed money" for certain ministries, or, asking for the right blessings, "ask not, have not" type of indoctrination and preaching, or expecting miracles as a sign of faith, we project the image as Christians, that because Christ has already overcome the world and sin, that the only thing left is for us to claim the victory. We seem to have forgotten, that while salvation is a free gift from God through Grace, it is not "free."

There is a requirement for salvation called the "sanctified life," or the living out of your faith based upon one's obedience and faithfulness t to the Word of God, through Self Sacrifice and Denial.", etc. People are reluctant to hear this other side of Grace, because it calls for the model of S**ervant hood**. We do not like being told what to do, not even by God himself. Man increasingly believes that he and he alone is the master of his ultimate destiny!

This world is not our home, but a temporary abode as finite and sinful creatures, separated from the fullness of God in this earthly flesh called the **body**. We are but sojourners in the **pilgrim** land of life here on earth. The life we live here is **not** our permanent dwelling place, as is alluded to in much of preaching today. Christ has gone to "prepare" a place in heaven for us when this life is **through**! This is the purpose of Jesus' death and resurrection as the only begotten Son of God the father – to save fallen humanity from the power of sin.

Unfortunately, however, the future as being with us is already reflected in our way of thinking as a society. This era is often referred to as a "Post Resurrection" society, in other words, as one that has moved beyond the saving works of the cross by Jesus! That event has now become a thing of the past, in today's "microwave society" of immediate gratification. "Today is all that counts."

The church, however, is not blameless for this condition. We are not preaching about the Wages of Sin, Hell and damnation for disobedience to God's Word, or faithfulness in living righteously, and the penalty for not. It is true that God is love and wants everybody to be saved, but the other side of love is retribution, or punishment! These things are not being preached today because the majority of people do not want to hear about what **we** should do to please God, while receiving his blessings.

Much of man's thoughts today are predicated on the belief that eventually, we will be able to do away with, or control to some extent, the death and dying process. One such endeavor is the so-called life support system, which is a machine said to prolong life. The name itself is a misnomer, because nothing can continue a life if is time for it to end! This life support system can only interfere with the natural dying process.

When a person is completely **dependent** upon a machine to breathe for them, and fail to survive when it is discontinued (called pulling the plug), it is because there is no quality of life left in that person.

There is a host of advertising today, about research surrounding the activity of being able to slow down, or prevent the deterioration of cells, for example, through genetic manipulation and gene splicing. These activities do nothing in controlling or altering the status of cells, including stem cell research and any other attempt to do so. The onset of **cloning for instance whether it is on animals, or possibly at some point humans are all exercises in futility.**

These attempts tend to deaden one's ability to trust and wait upon the natural order of things, that are outside of man's in control. The emphasis on manmade ideologies, diminish our ability to plan and wait for God's timeline for life. This is why focusing on the future of eternal life as promised to us by God, becomes so increasingly difficult for man to do.

An example of a deadening tradition that weakens life instead of strengthening it is the continuing influence that the past JimCrow ideology, still has on the black community concerning higher education. The time is long past that this millstone be broken.

This deadening tradition speaks to us today about how we as blacks have allowed the **voice of the past**, to cause higher education to become a strange bedfellow in the black community, by attaching black and white connotations to it. **We have no one to blame but ourselves!**

I was a victim myself during the 70's of the truth of this statement. I pastored over 30 years in the United Methodist church, a predominately white denomination, and was very comfortable with being the only black minister wherever I went. As a large black former Marine, football and basketball player, with a big afro hairstyle and a heavy, deep voice, which I acknowledged could be somewhat intimidating to those who did not know me, were of minimal concern in my pastoring.

When I retired from the pastorate after thirty or so years to become a chaplain in a large predominately white hospital in Ohio, I was being trained in CPE (clinical pastoral education) to become a full time certified chaplain. During one of my classes, I was described by a small, elderly, Catholic Nun also a student in the program, as being huge, intimidating and frightening, and one who would not make a successful hospital chaplain because, I would make patients uncomfortable in my presence, which she described as over powering.

After completing my training six months later, I expressed my feelings to my on sight supervisor from my counseling center, about feeling that I did not belong in the hospital as a chaplain, even after all of my pastoral experience, basically remembering what this Nun said about me in class. My supervisor told me that he had talked to numerous staff persons and patients in the hospital about my work.

He informed me that he had not received anything but positive feedback about me! After undergoing counseling, he made me aware that what was said about me in the past, had no bearing on me today, because I was not that person today, because I had learned to minimize my size and intimidating presence once I was made aware of them.

I had learned to forge new images of myself from past experiences, but needed to be aware that I was not that same person perceived earlier. I had to learn to accept myself as I was now. He made me aware that I was being haunted by voices of the past! When we free ourselves from these past experiences, we are no longer allowing past institutional structures to rule over us, and prevent us from creating new and greater experiences for us today.

We hear constantly as black folk talk to each other, that we are still in bondage or slavery, but only in a new form! The essence of this statement is a form of **mental bondage**, which contains no bars or cells, but is the hardest prison to escape from because this bondage is self-imposed!

Some whites today wish that the past could be resurrected, but the dead does not come back to life. If racism and prejudice exist today, it does so only the minds and hearts of those who refuse to accept the march of time and the changes that it brings. It is a dead tradition. I acknowledge that the ghosts of times past can haunt us much longer than they need to.

We blacks have got to realized that God has granted us a new beginning as a people, but he will not do for us what we need to do for ourselves. God provides food for the birds but does not drop the worms in their nests! When they leave the nest to hunt for their food, this is what gives rise to the phrase "the early bird gets the worm."

We need to first become more assertive as individuals about our educational opportunities, and then pass this trait on to our children. This is not only a cultural imperative, but an individual one first. Each black person must realize that this task must fall on the shoulder of every single individual if it is to happen.

Slavery and racism are hand me down traditions that we have revolted against with moral justification and should overcome. The question is, when? It becomes very frustrating to see how we as blacks continue to crawl along at a snail's pace, while limiting ourselves from moving forward, because we refuse to think for ourselves as a people. It almost appears as though we are waiting for another leader to come along and take us by the hand.

I have always believed that everything done in darkness will soon come to the light. One clear example of this in the educational process is the way in which the history books have been rewritten in the past thirty years or so, to reflect how blacks have contributed to the wellbeing of this nation. Hypocrisy has its cost and is like any other lie that only last for a season until before being exposed.

The repudiation, unfortunately, of higher education among other things in the black community, is really the end result of the rejection of a previous corporate structure that offered little or no hope to black America, even in the area of education. It's oppressive and demeaning treatment of its own people in light of the guaranteed promises to all in the constitution is a mockery of justice!

This hypocrisy was, and still is, such a travesty that it has threatened the whole future of trust in this nation! Even much our youth has lost confidence in the country, and it enjoys only meager support of the rest. This is the terrible **penalty** now being paid in our society. No amount of remorse, regret, and shame can undo the harm that has been done. Our society must now live with the shame of what it has done, in spite of millions that wish that somehow it would just away.

The problem with sin and lies is that they don't just disappear. Once an evil is done, it makes an indelible mark that will last forever. It's like saying something that you wish you could retract, but can't. Once something is said, it cannot be taken back because someone else has already heard it! This is the way that moral evils suffer. Once they have been committed, they last forever in the minds of those affected.

I believed that millions of people in this generation today, who were not a part and parcel of causing these unfortunate sins of the past, wish that in some way they would just disappear, especially our young people who simply just don't understand what's behind the dynamics of things that they do, but which persuade or dictate the way that they behave, like ridiculing their classmates in college for placing more of an emphasis on study than "hanging out."

The end result in the final analysis of this problem is a loss of confidence and trust in our system, with a lack of tolerance in it as well. This lack of tolerance in the mind of the present generation is evident in the sense of impatience that is obvious in today's generation. These are some of the most frustrating things that the older generation experiences.

We have lived through these atrocities and evils, and can look back and see the progress that has been made in our society, realizing that much more is still needed to take place. But the younger generation can only see what needs to be changed, and this progress is moving at a snail's pace. They ask the question "how much longer do we have to wait before things get better?"

Here is where historical films and documentations such as the civil rights struggles of the 60's and 70's serve to educate youth. As ludicrous as it seems, our young folk today are not aware for the most part, of the unsavory conduct of previous generations. When parents attempt to tell their children about them their words are seen as "mom and dad are just old fashioned and don't understand what's happening." We are often dismissed as irrelevant.

Most parents today are painfully aware of how frustrating it is, of trying to get our children to listen to us, just as it was for our parents to get us to listen to them when we were young. What goes around comes around! The distrust and alienation of a whole generation has been lost. So the million dollar question is "how then is trust restored?"

For every action there is an opposite and equal reaction, and I believe that this principle was overlooked by white America in the early stages of this situation. This has led to the current dilemma of the role of higher education in the life of black Americans. Our current President Barack Obama, a black man, has not changed this unfortunate condition. With his election, much still needs to be done and changed.

In his state of the union address this year in2013, he highlighted the experience of the black teenager killed by a grown middle age

white man, who was later exonerated in court as Self Defense. The president said that thirty years ago the boy killed could have been him. Then he recounted in his own life how he, like numerous other black males including myself, would be followed in a department store by detectives from the time we entered until the time we left.

The average black American has a tendency to see his election as some sort of a utopian experience for black folk. While it is a significant step forward for America, it has the handprint of God all over it, just as the life and work of MLK JR's life had, but still falls woefully short of the American dream.

To call attention as to why trust is so difficult to restore, one only needs to look at the ingenious ways that man devises to disguise his true feelings. The invention of the **glass ceiling** is only one example of this. Since it is no longer legal to discriminate in hiring on the basis of religion, nationality or gender in the workplace, this concept was conceived.

The Glass Ceiling is still the pervading ideology in the work place, designed to maintain the status quo of the white male at the top of the corporate ladder! It is an ingenuous devise, however, which only highlights man's ability to disguise his true intentions in order to protect his own assets! Since you can no longer discriminate in the workplace based upon nationality, religion, and gender, other means need to be concocted to accomplish this.

However, let me clarify the reality of this, because I want to give credit where credit is due. This is a NEW time and generation in which we live, and in prior generations, white America did not see the need to pacify Black Americans. This is just a sign that many changes have taken place in our society, and they need to be noted.

Even in the midst of this, one thing still remains to be discussed, and that is the difference in the glass ceiling between the black male intellectual and his female intellectual counterpart. If you notice and pay attention to the difference, black women are still more advanced in the work place than the black male (this is my personal observation).

A black woman fills **two** roles in the workplace, (a female and a minority). This affects the statistical analysis that companies are hiring not only females, but blacks as well. One of the problems that this has created within the black family is that many females are out producing her husband in income and this has caused a crisis within the family.

This is not all inclusive, but is a common reality. Of all minorities in this country, the black male still remains at the bottom of the social structure. If you notice, inter racial marriages are more acceptable between whites and any other minority other than with blacks. I believe that this is due to the history of slavery in this country. Nobody wants to be lower than the black American!

All of these dynamics are in the black American's physic, especially the black male intellectual! Black males have always known that the black female has been more acceptable in white America than the male, going all the way back to slavery when black women often raised the children of their white slave masters, and many times became the mistress of the white slave owners, often bearing their illegitimate children!

Many of the young black Americans are not fully aware of these issues because they have never been taught or made aware of them in the history books. This is why the current crop of black parents and grandparents need to take the initiative. Unfortunately this is not happening as much as it should.

Here is where black America needs to be more responsible with its own destiny. White America is not solely responsible to change the destiny of its black citizens! This is **our** responsibility as black folk! If you wait for others to solve your problems you are exhibiting childlike behavior. Regardless of the past, we as blacks are responsible to solve our own problems, whether we get help doing it or not!

CHAPTER SIX

Fixing the problem

The black male's responsibility

Let's not duck and dodge the issue here. This book is specifically about the plight of the black American intellectual, no more, no less. Let's keep the main thing the main thing! The individual responsible to fix this problem rests mainly on the shoulders of the black intellectual, along with the help of the **entire** black community as well! There is no need to be sidetracked by secondary issues that will not resolve the problem, such as the past racism of Jim Crow laws, the former slave issue, the glass ceiling problem, the racial climate today in America, etc., etc. **This is a black problem plain and simple!**

The persons responsible to alter or change this problem within the black community as a whole, in a corporate sense, lay with every black person. The black intellectual did not cause or create this dilemma, and it cannot exist without being aided and abetted in some sense by black folk as well. In many ways we have allowed this situation to continue by allowing the conditions that created this problem to manifest themselves within us mentally, and create a sense of apathy and Self Defeatist attitudes about education as stated previously.

No laws made by others, should allow persons to become a prisoner unto themselves **The first thing that must be done in**

order to rectify the disparity in education between the black and white communities is to see it for what it is. It can no longer be ignored or swept under the rug. Black folk must accept their part for allowing external factors to control their innermost being.

We are only limited by our own selves. Black folk have allowed these **conditions to become a type of neurosis,** which understood in this context as a mental disorder which results in an abnormally intense apathy leading to a resentment toward these limitations, and blaming white folk for them by applying illogical perceptions such as being "whitewashed" by the white man's educational system.

Here is where black Americans need to apply introspection to our frailties, without searching for a scapegoat to cover them up! Self Examination is always an extremely difficult thing to do because it involves looking at oneself instead of others. We need instead to learn the dynamics as blacks of adaptability to break this neurosis. This is **our** problem and our problem only.

We have failed to adapt to the change of the times. How many times have we heard about the necessity of change? Nature teaches us that in order to survive, animals need to adapt to their environment. People are no different. If we don't change, we get left behind, and that is what's happening to blacks today. We are still carrying around left over and out dated baggage.

Harold O.J. Brown talks about two kinds of changes that take place in humans. One of them is Static adaption, when people fail to make necessary changes in order to move on, and therefore remain the same. This can be seen as an example in the alcoholic who wants to obtain sobriety, but refuses to throw away the bottle.

Static adaption in blacks

This **static adaption** can be seen in the black community with the acceptance that higher education will only have **limited** results for blacks. This has led black Americans to become passive and

lacking in Self Confidence, resulting in accepting these perceived limitations as **determining**! This is the essence of apathy and is no one's fault but our own! When this happens, we allow others to dictate the past to us, and thus control the direction of our future! In essence, we build a man- made prison for ourselves with no one to blame but ourselves!

Blacks have fallen into this category of a **static** sense of adaption, because our mindset has remained pretty much the same way without change concerning education, because of the inequities of the past which we have yet to overcome! Let me cite at least one example.

In1970, I entered a black university for the first time as an older student of twenty five years of age, having spent four years in the Marine Corp. The **GI educational Bill** was my ticket to a college education. At that time you could count the number of black college students on the finger of one hand in your neighborhood. It was a brand new experience for the most part, and blacks did not really have a sense of what was going on, which was acceptable at the time.

Upper level career opportunities for African Americans were severely limited or practically nonexistent. There was little or no encouragement to pursue a higher education except for the few who saw the forest in spite of the trees. I was very disappointed with the conduct of the black students on campus with their irresponsible and often belligerent attitudes about school.

I admit that most of them were eighteen and nineteen year old freshmen, and I was a more mature adult, but no one had to tell you to study after classes were over. The library was usually empty, while large crowds gathered on the steps of the dorms with vulgar language emanating from them, and loud music was blasting all over the campus. This happened **every** day! The few black students who chose to study instead of following the crowd were ridiculed.

Students would habitually come late to class, often chewing wads of gum, knowing that chewing gum was prohibited in the classroom, and then were sullen and disrespectful to the instructor when this was brought to their attention. Some students even showed up to class in pajamas and shower shoes! Many of the male students had Afro picks sticking out of their hair, and some female students were braless and barely covered.

The teacher many times had to talk over classroom noise and clowning around among the students. Absenteeism was always a problem. Many parents would have been appalled at seeing how their hard earned dollars were going to waste with their children's behavior. This was when higher education was in its infancy in the black community **fifty** years or so ago!

I said all of this to make a point. Since 1970, over fifty years ago, little has changed in the attitudes of black college students. All one has to do is dare to ask any college professor or professional in our black universities as to the state of affairs in their schools. I have talked with several black college professors and professional in churches I have pastored, and still receive confirmation concerning these matters.

What really disturbs me more than any one single factor is the **lack** of **progress** we have made as a people since then. It is tragic but true, that the "static adaption" label is a reality among us today, even though more blacks than ever are receiving college degrees. As a race, we still lack on an individual basis the intestinal fortitude to be change makers, not only as individuals, but collectively.

In many ways, America has matured as a nation, in spite of all the things yet to be done. It appears as though we are still waiting for another charismatic leader or savior like Martin Luther King, Jr, to appear and chart a new course of action and direction for us a people. Fifty years after his civil rights movement in this country, he would be appalled at the state of the union among African Americans when examining the nature of our character as highlighted in the **Critique of Blackness** mentioned earlier.

How can it be that in spite of all the cultural and racial changes that has been made in this country since then, that we have still lagged so far behind as a culture? If we want to continue lamenting about what is wrong with America, as a way of refusing to let go of the past, which some of us still use as an excuse for antisocial behaviors, we are doomed to remain a stagnant or static people!

No matter how much still remains to be done in our nation, it **cannot** be denied that much has been accomplished on practically all fronts. Our immigration patterns have become as such that Hispanics are now the most numerous ethnic group in the country. We have become a beacon of religious diversity, and racial tolerance now sees a record number of interracial relationships and marriages, racial slurs have now been relegated to using abbreviations, rather than name calling the "N' rather than the word "nigger". All major Universities are now fully integrated even in the Deep South

As I stated earlier, it's frustrating to understand why we as black folk can't see the forest for the trees. Is it so hard to understand how getting an advanced degree in college can be a detriment to us instead of advancing us? Education is designed to help us grow not only into adulthood, but to help make us grow into better persons!

This is why I get so frustrated. More black now than ever have received or are receiving college educations, and yet we seem to be making little or no progress in our cultural maturation. We still practice so many self defeatist behaviors and ways of thinking! It's difficult to understand why we have become our own worst enemy. Look at the outrageous black on black murders and drug use, which we cannot point the finger at white society any longer!

When are we going to **grow up** and see what we are doing to our own selves? With one of every three young African American males expected to be locked up before the age of thirty, coupled with the exorbitant murder rate, we are committing racial **Genocide among ourselves!** How can we not see this? Whether we like it or not, it only reflects our adolescent way of thinking, which begs to grow into adulthood as a people.

If we cannot see for ourselves what is in our best interest as persons, who then is responsible for our blindness? Even without being told, our youth should be able to understand for themselves, that any time I grow in knowledge, I am becoming a better person and individual, regardless of whatever obstacles still need to be removed. Two things that marked my life were taught to me by mother when I was child; "The only way that someone can be better than you is that they are a better person;" and secondly, "Remember, if someone else can do it, so can you!"

Dynamic adaption in blacks

This is what Brown refers to when one changes old behaviors and patterns in order to establish new directions and goals for themselves. When my brother and I, who is a year younger than I am, received a college education back in the 70's, we were the first siblings in the history of our family to do so.

Now, many of our children and Grand Children are receiving college educations, and the result is that going to college after high school is expected whenever possible, and is becoming a family trait! When this happens, the intestinal fortitude of the individual becomes of paramount importance. If you expect something to change, you must do something to make it happen.

When a family changes it's mindset from not going to college to being expected to go to college, then the family physic has been changed! This is how a family curse is broken! There is a saying which goes, "if you always do what you've always done, you will always get what you've always gotten."

This change is what Brown refers to as Dynamic Adaption. This is where we as a race need to be if we are going to mature as we should. When a person desires to change an event, they must arrive at a point where the current direction being traveled is no longer acceptable, and new conduct and ways of thinking must occur. When this takes place, then the reality of change, as the author states below is ready to begin in earnest.

The motivation to change

The hostility that causes blacks not to change in this particular situation is **unresolved** or repressed anger that blacks feel, which has been allowed to become dormant and cancerous! This hostility stems from the residual effects of racism and prejudice against blacks over the years, which has not been successfully dealt with, and therefore leads to the current dilemma that this work addresses.

This is the place where the eventual solution to the problem must be found and take place! Here is where the rubber meets the road! **Blacks are angry** and we need to acknowledge and own up to it, rather than to bury our heads in the sand and accept it passively. This is the Psychological disorder known as T**ransference** {where a problem which one has, is transferred to another as if it's **their** problem, and then reacting to it as such).

Because this problem has not been resolved, its residual effect is fleshed out in the dilemma created by blacks against whites, in the form of distrusting the opportunity of a higher education to be seen as self advancement, other than as the **perceived** vehicle for controlling us, thus becoming what some refer to as being "whitewashed!" This perception is of our own making, and not that of white folk! We need to stop blaming others for our problems.

This hostility in our case is that it becomes a dynamic factor in our character structure as a people. Everything in life is a continuum, where one thing affects another. We are the sum of all of our parts. One cannot isolate one event from another as if they are compartmentalized. While we combat the issues of racial discrimination, it cannot be disassociated from the problem with education. One has everything to do with the other!

D**isequilibrium,** which is the state of having one's comfort zone disturbed, is the seedbed of growth. In blacks this is the undisturbed issue of our anger. Only when the status quo becomes unacceptable does the need to change happen. It is when our comfort zone is attacked do we see the need to change. This is where the major role of the black male intellectual needs to take center stage, and the black community to take heed to their scholarly critique!

When this comfort zone is attacked, it produces a new anxiety which leads to a new vague defiance as stated by brown earlier. This new defiance is in the form of rejecting our previous passive acceptance of limitations perceived or actual, imposed upon us by white society. When this happens, we are now becoming our own critical thinkers and thus maturing as a people!

Rather than rejecting changes or ridiculing the individuals who are calling for these changes, we as mature people must now be open to Self Examination and change if we are to move forward. One of the hardest things for individuals to accept is to see the need to change. This is to acknowledge our faults and shortcomings, which are blows to our pride and egos.

Too many of us suffer from **illusions of Grandeur** (pretentiously pompous ways of thinking) including blacks in the form of anti-social behaviors. Another lesson from my childhood says; "never let your pride make a fool out of you!" Pride can often be a cover for anger.

White Responsibility for change

This problem can no longer be swept under the rug or covered up! White America must accept the responsibility for creating this problem, as well as the black community for allowing it to exist and have an effect on its psyche. As strange as it may appear, **both** sides will be charged with the responsibility of bringing it to a close. Playing the blame game will be an exercise in futility, because the current generation did not create the problem, but it **is** responsible for finding a solution.

It may be tempting for whites to try and blame the victims for this dilemma, using the rationale that whites are not responsible for the mindset of blacks concerning education. After all, they are responsible for the way they think? This may have **some** merit in the sense that we do assume ownership of our own thinking, but this only leads to the realization that we are all affected by the past, and the way in which we were raised!

The problem with education and the perception of it in the black community is the **residual** effect of prior discrimination and deceit. The lasting effects of these ills and shortcomings initially were not for seeable. However, let us be clear about this, as hindsight is always 20 20! White America is now beginning to understand the magnitude of what they created fifty some years ago.

The Apostle Paul tells us in the Bible that "when I was a child, I spoke as a child, but when I became a man I put away childish things!" There comes a time when an adult must be held accountable for their own thinking. An adult at some point must stop blaming their parents for the way they were raised, as an excuse for lack of their own adult behavior. This is the challenge for black America today as it relates to higher education!

Continuing the gains made

It is undeniable that great strides have been made in America's race relations over the past fifty years between blacks and whites. Middle to older generations of Americans have witnessed and experienced these changes in their own lifetime. For one, it was unforeseeable fifty years ago that a black American male would become president of this country, let alone be elected to a second term! These gains are just emblematic of the progress that has been made.

The truth of these realities rest in what I call the naivety of the current generation of young black people who do not understand how this ludicrous racial problem had gotten to be so bad. Primarily, this is because they have not lived through it or experienced it first hand, yet it has always been present! It is one thing to hear about something and another to live it. Because of this, it **is** necessary to expatiate at great length about this phenomenon.

Brown is absolutely correct in stating that the will of God calls for reconciliation, because all mankind comes from **his** creative hand. **We are all God's children,** and because of this, his will is that we should all be reconciled with one another as one family. After all, there is really only **one** race, and that is the human race which by divine creation is the only one family on earth!

One of the major problems today with the secular mind is that religion is often ignored in the final solution of human inner relationships. This leads to a multitude of varying dispositions and philosophies that in most cases are in conflict with each other. Yet in spite of all our shortcomings, progress with race relations continues to be made, however slowly.

However, we cannot rest on our laurels because there still are so many problems and obstacles that we need to overcome. A word of caution need to be given to those with a false sense of euphoria because of the gains made. Some are attempting to say that because of them we no longer need the laws of the past that ensured these.

There are calls today by some to repel them based on the assumption that this is a new age, and that these old laws infringe on the civil rights of the first amendment of the Constitution for the current generation. What a thinly disguised excuse for attempting to turn back the clock.

The truth of this statement is undeniable in its entirety. The only way to build a truly just society is one built in love which is unselfish, and completely devoid of all exploitation and arrogance on the behalf of everyone involved. If enough Americans have the courage and intestinal fortitude to do this regardless of color, and have the courage to stand up and be counted, then this panacea of a complete just society can become a reality.

This involves much more than to simply disclaim the ills of the past that such a shakedown would involve. **Because of courageous people like those mentioned above, more blacks are now receiving a college education than ever before.** This trend must continue at all cost, because the dilemma of education being a strange bedfellow in the black community is a distinct reality. Whether we want to accept it or not, there are still plenty of folk today who long for the return of the old days.

This is clearly evident by the influx of information coming from the media about the back lash of the election of President Obama, the first black president of this country, coming in the form of new ideologies and forms of racism that are no longer overt, but covert!

It is no longer legal to prevent blacks from voting today, but the new forms of voting registration and ID requirements, are clearly racist, and intended to do the most harm to poor and indigenous blacks and other minorities. Attempts to overturn the civil rights legislations of the 60's and 70's have begun to rear their ugly heads.

Unless the heart of a man is changed, everything else will always remain the same. You can take a pig, give him a bath, spray him with perfume, put a suit of clothes on him, sit him in a brand new car, and you still have nothing but a dressed up pig sitting in a car, because he still has the **mind** of pig! There's an old saying which says that you can take a person out of the ghetto, but you can't take the ghetto out of the person.

Racism is still very much alive and kicking in America, in spite of gains that have been made recently, because the heart of racial prejudice still remain in many people. Martin Luther King's civil rights dream for this nation as one brotherhood with love and justice for everyone has still yet to be accomplished, even with the election of its first African American president! Do not be misled, this is not a panacea!

Today much has changed to a great degree with the influx of other nationalities and races, much for the better. Today, Muslim Mosques are springing up all over the country, and religious diversity is thriving. Hispanics and Spanish speaking persons are now the majority populations. This is a good thing for our country, which after all is a nation of emigrants from all parts of the world. The only American not an emigrant is the Native American (Indians).

For the first time whites in this country are experiencing a sense of loss, and the feeling of losing control, as well as the erosion of power. With the powerful dividing lines among the races being diminished, unadulterated racism and ethnic hatred seems to somehow be slowly disappearing, and must continue by any means possible!. This challenge facing the nation is a new experience for most of them, but it is a price that must be paid.

Sooner or later our sins catch up to us with a price that must be satisfied in order to move on. Everything in life comes with a price tag attached to it. There is nothing free in life! We may not like or agree with the price that must be paid, that should have been considered **first** before we commit the transgression.

Now we as a nation must try and figure out what must be done to change the mistakes made in the past, and many of us are not going to like or appreciate the price that must be paid. Scores of folk will simply refuse to pay it. Ironically, many of these same people had little or no problem accepting these sins when they were being done. Of course, this is the height of hypocrisy and conceit.

The primary problem encountered here is that the solution is not one sided. If whites strive to overcome and change the errors of the past, black must be willing to accept their overtures. The problem is that it is difficult for blacks to accept efforts from white America as truly being sincere, when all you have known your entire life is lies, deceit and hatred!

When there is this amount of historical distrust, bigotry, hatred, and racial manipulation, how can the scars heal in a normal fashion? The answer lies beyond the reach of what ordinary people think, because the solution will call for extra ordinary measures. Whites and blacks have never trusted one another enough to make a true difference in this area, and this is what complicates this matter beyond human comprehension.

What then is the answer? Let's now examine a suggested solution by white scholar Harold O.J. Brown cited below, in his book **Christianity and the class struggle o**ver 45 years ago, and which appears to be prophetic. The solution to the problem he introduced was amalgamated rapid interbreeding much to the chagrin of many people, black and white, but which appears to be the only real solution to the problem.

When you look at athletes for example, it is often difficult to tell at first glance whether they are black or white. Tiger Woods and Lolo Jones are two examples. Tiger looks black, but Lolo does not. Both have mixed parents and are therefore neither black nor white. When this is the case, identifying people based on appearances becomes a mute issue, and this is a positive rather thing than a detriment. This tends to minimize the temptation by certain individuals to discriminate, and practice prejudicial behavior based on appearance.

Those of us old enough to remember what happened to singer Doris Day in the 1960's, witnessed one of the most convincing arguments of this matter. She was one of the most popular figures in the entertainment world passed off as white by appearance. When it was discovered that she had a black grandparent, her career and popularity hit rock bottom instantaneously, and she was finished.

Interbreeding

This concept as a means of breaking down some of the apparent racial physical appearances of the races, will at least retard the immediate dispensation of racism, because of the blurred physical characteristics that interbreeding will do. This is a bitter pill for us to swallow, but it appears that this is the best solution to this problem!

We can see this happening all around us today. Interracial dating and marriages are almost common place now. When you stop to consider the fact that just over thirty years ago In America, it was **against the law** in Virginia for blacks and whites to marry each other! They would actually be breaking the law and convicted of a crime and sentenced to jail or prison!

This is how bad racism, Jim Crow laws, and injustice to blacks had become for those too young to know that this existed. Years ago before such bigotry and hatred became the accepted way of living you could watch little preschool children black and white, playing together having a great time. Their color made no difference to them at all.

It was not until they grew older and began to go to school and were now apart from each other, that they were exposed to racial hatred, and became indoctrinated with prejudice and bigotry by parents, and other adults, that their friendships were destroyed by propaganda and myths based on lies.

Let me cite one example of this from my own experience, and I know that many others can relate to similar experiences in their lives. When I pastored in the United Methodist Church during the 1970's, I was a camp counselor in our conference in West Ohio.

I was one of only a handful of black ministers in the conference. We met at a district camp meeting one month as district leaders, to discuss possible ways to teach the kids how to combat this form of bigotry. I worked as a high school counselor.

Our strategy was to form an interracial camp with black and white students within the conference. We chose to select kids from an inner city black neighborhood and whites from a predominately white suburban community from another city, and put them together. This was in part the brainchild of the forced bussing strategy by the government to end the segregation of public schools.

Each camp would have their own set of counselors from their area, led by ordained pastors as camp directors and laypersons as support staff. The camp was held at a facility owned by the church. We knew that we were blazing new ground in church relationships, after acknowledging that the most segregated day in America was on Sunday mornings, and we were determined to address the issue as leaders. In order to make a change you must begin somewhere.

When the camp came together in a large assembly hall on the camp ground, just as we leaders suspected, each group segregated themselves at opposite ends of the building. After introducing ourselves, we asked the kids to look around and tell us what they saw. After a long period of silence, one white youth commented about the visible racial separation of the camp. Then another student said that this doesn't seem much like a church camp, because Christians should not be apart like this. This was the ice breaker we leaders were looking for. Several others on both sides then began to open up about their personal experiences.

After that, the rest was easy. We announced that all of the activities of a camp would be done together as one group. We then encouraged them to talk to each other where they sat. Many of them confessed that they had not been around the other, and many had no blacks or whites in their communities. What they knew of each other was by word of mouth from others and what they saw on television.

We followed this up by having them eat together at integrated dinner tables. This gave them the opportunity to share intimately. You could actually feel the thawing in their relationships beginning to happen. Sporting activity between the two groups went extremely well as they played with one another. Here is where we encountered our biggest challenges, with dancing, music and the sharing of the swimming pool.

First let's start with the music. Black kids did not like a lot of the country and western music of the white kids, and the whites did not like a lot of the soul music of the blacks. When the music of each group was played, they did not dance to the other's music. We asked them why not, many of them claimed that they did not feel the beat, yet both types of music had drums, guitars, horns, etc.

We told them that the music itself had nothing to do with it, but rather it was the attitudes about it. They then shared with us the things that they were taught by their parents and others of how and why to dislike the other's style of music.

We leaders and counselors demonstrated to them by dancing to whatever music was played. Shortly afterwards, both groups were dancing to each other's music without any problems. Like the forced bussing issue, this goes to prove that sometimes the races needed to be coaxed and encouraged to interact with each other with **adult** supervision.

The next thing that we tackled was the swimming pool issue. We noticed that each group would not get in the pool together. We challenged them to explain why not. As they shared with us, we learned some very interesting things.

The white kids were taught that if they shared a swimming pool with blacks, that the color of the black kids would get in their skin and turn them black, and that black also urinated in the pool and often left excrement or feces in the pool.

The black kids were taught the same things about the whites, except that their color would not come off, but that when whites get wet, they smell like dogs, and that the odor would get on them. One just as bad as the other!

Where there is no other framework of reference in which to base a responsible decision, one is prone to accepting that which they are exposed to. This is the plight that children faced of being indoctrinated by those persons that they trusted and looked up to.

Again, we as leaders were forced to demonstrate to the kids that these were false and misleading things that they were taught, by getting into the pool with both black and whites, proving the falsehood of these allegations. Again, the example of **adult** leadership is crucial to the upbringing of our children. In short order, needless to say, both groups shared the same pool, at the same time, without incident.

For ten days the kids had a wonderful time together. On the next to the last day of the camp, we gathered all the kids together as we did when the camp first started. This time, however, they all sat together. We told them that they would have to say their goodbyes to each other. This is where the shock happened for us counselors and leaders, as well as the entire camp itself.

While saying their goodbyes to each other, the most dramatic love fest that I had ever witnessed took place. Black and white kids together began to cry, sob and hug one another noisily and without shame. The noise was so loud, that the administrators of the camp thought that there was trouble and came to investigate.

What they found was a scene reminiscent of a mini day of Pentecost, where the Holy Spirit was reigning supreme! That's why I know for myself, that when God is in control, people **can** together be an **automaton** (one body sharing an identical experience and cause) as Erich Fromm states in his book **Escape from freedom.**

Next we were faced with our biggest challenge, getting the kids ready for their return trips home with their parents who were coming to pick them up. We knew that we would have to deprogram the kids from the experience that they had learned at camp, because they had learned firsthand the lies and falsehoods of the things that they had been told.

The first thing that we told them was that their parents would not understand their experience, and that it would be a waste of time trying to explain it, other than blacks and whites could get along with each other just as the Bible teaches that all people should love one another.

We cautioned them to be ready for what would happen when their parents came to pick them up, and see them saying goodbye to their new found friends. They should not harbor ill feelings toward their parents, when they would express their anger and disappointment at what they saw, because this was totally foreign to the way they were raised. Their parents would then learn from them the same falsehoods and lies that they themselves were taught.

Let them know that they were loved the same as they were always loved before. The best way to teach them is by example. Whenever they encountered racism from then on just let the others know that they did not agree with them, and would not to participate in racist activity or any kind.

When their parents did arrive to pick them up, the anger was visible on their faces as they drove way with tires squealing!

We as leaders were over joyed that we had the wisdom and foresight to deprogram them, and prepare the kids to reenter the real world of realism, as opposed to the ideal world that the Bible teaches, about the way that the world should be experienced.

Black responsibility

It is imperative that we as blacks recognize our role in the continuation of these gains and by our participation in them as a race. We **must** step up to the plate and assume our **adult** responsibility as a mature culture, no longer rejecting positive criticism, and seeking to make excuses for our lack of initiative and fortitude.

This results in creating our own sense of change and Self Understanding, along with the acceptance of our weaknesses, thereby becoming our own mature change agent.

This means getting rid of creating our own misconceptions, while overcoming the problems between our cultures, and seeing the importance of higher education for ourselves. This is something that no one else can do for us. We cannot live in the past, as it will destroy our ability to live in the present and plan for the future. This is when we will have arrived as adults as a people, putting away childish misconceptions and influences.

Mutual commitment to enact change

The first thing that must be done is to eliminate the blame game. Whites want to blame blacks and blacks want to blame whites. This is an exercise in futility, because no single race is solely responsible for this condition. The Second thing that needs to happen is that every single person must accept responsibility for making a change. One person may not be able to solve this problem by themselves, but they are at least **one,** and can help make a change one person at a time.

In order to make a corporate change in our society, every individual must make a personal change, and sacrifice for the good of the whole. Only when we have the good of the other person at heart, can there ever be such a thing as mutual commitment and trust between individuals.

This is the responsibility of **both** parties involved. Mutual trust can only evolve when the individual gives up himself in a type of sacrificial offering, for the sake of creating something new. This means that the individual now becomes a part of a **corporate** reality for change! Here is where the problem lies. It means that in order to truly solve the race problem we face at this time, and to establish a new order, we as a people must be on one accord.

In order not to spin our wheels, we need to stop treating the **symptoms** of racism by applying Band-Aids to open wounds! This is done by trying to simply eliminate the word "nigger" for instance, with the use of the "N" word! This is not working today and will never work, even at the time of this writing, without removing the **root cause** of the problem, which is simply the racial hatred of blacks!

You cannot Legislate morality and bring about significant changes. With all of the civil rights legislation of the past fifty years, racism is still alive and well. Let me attempt to diffuse this issue as much as I am able to do.

When I grew up as a child in the 1950's, every ethnic group had its own neighborhood in Columbus, Ohio, my home town. All of these groups lived in their own homogenous communities, the German Americans, Italian Americans, French Americans, Jewish Americans, African Americans, etc.

Each group was labeled with a racial slur meant to demean. I will attempt to spell these slur names correctly, but since they do not exist in the dictionary, I'll try and use them as we called them at that time. Blacks were called (Niggers), Italians(Wops), Spanish speaking persons(Wetbacks}, Germans, (Krauts}, Polish,(Polocks), Japanese(Japs),Chinese(Chinks}, Whites(Honkies), British(Lymies) etc.

Over time, these terms were reduced to be simply labels, having lost their original demeaning intent, primarily because they did not contain elements of racial hatred except for the word "nigger." **This word is the exception to the rule**!

No other group of immigrants were treated and abused as the former slaves were. This hatred and contempt for American blacks, eventually caused the nation to be divided over the slavery issue (the civil war), where brothers, fathers, sisters and relatives, fought each other over this. This war has never been overcome in the hearts of millions.

This hatred has existed and survived for so long, that it is no longer an issue of race or color, but a systemic reality of our society. It is engrained into the fabric of American society to the extent that even though it may not be fully understood by those who have not experienced it firsthand, it nonetheless is an expected and intuitive way of thinking that people expect others to feel.

This tugs at the heart of the current generation of our youth, who do not feel or experience the hatred and contempt of their parents do about racial relations, but are taught them nonetheless. This creates ambiguity and confusion in the minds of our young folk. That's why being called a nigger today, while still offensive and derogatory, does not carry the same weight as it used to.

With the proliferation of interracial dating and marriages that take place today, how do you expect these youngsters to comprehend fully why a law making such a relationship **illegal** and against the law to begin with? It is little wonder why black youth today cannot fully understand why receiving a college education is not always a desirable thing, and why this dilemma even exists.

Erich Fromm mentioned in the early 70's a concept of **automation conformity**, as a means in which to establish a just and loving society based upon a universal common goal, thus becoming an **automated** society, made up entirely of what he calls the **automation** of each individual. This means that he becomes identical with millions of other

Here is where the problem arises. This is a high price to pay for the average person, and the giving up of self is a sacrifice that few if any, are willing to make! We are taught all of our lives to become an individual thinker, and most of us are reluctant to give this up. We are taught not to become an automated thinker as Fromm alludes to here. However, in order to eliminate this dilemma concerning racism and blackness in higher education, this is exactly what needs to take place.

We as a collective people must see the need to prioritize this enough in order to become automated as individuals, eventually becoming an automated society! This need corroborates what Brown has stated earlier, that race hatred cannot be cooled off except by racial amalgamation in rapid interbreeding. Both of these scholars are saying essentially the same thing, just in a different way.

What this does is to blur or minimize racial distinctions, which creates these problems in the first place, by creating a society of **mixed racial individuals,** that often cannot readily be identified as one race or the other. We can see that this is beginning to happen before our very eyes today unless we're blind. In other words, racial hatred needs to be overcome in order to establish an automated society where all are working for the same end.

In this particular situation, the elimination of dissolving the current dilemma of higher education in blackness, finds the solution not in the individual thought processes, but in the collective thinking of the masses aimed at accomplishing a certain cause that will be acceptable. This is what it means to become an automated society, coupled with the amalgamation of rapid interbreeding, appear to be the only solutions to the problem at hand.

The major obstacle to overcome here appears to be the commitment of every individual involved to be willing to give up enough of their sense of self autonomy, for the good of society as a whole. This is as foreign to mankind as loving your enemies regardless of how they treat you, as the scriptures admonish us to do. Each of us if we are honest will admit that without the help of divine intervention, this seems to be an impossibility to accomplish, much as it is presented here.

CHAPTER SEVEN

Summary

In summary, this is what has been discussed. In Chapter One, we looked at this dilemma from a historical perspective. The genesis of racial hatred of course dates back to slavery, where blacks were not considered to be fully human beings. This was continued for generations with the **proof texting** (explained later), of the biblical account of the different races on earth, with the **Tower of Babel** account in the Old Testament. In order to stop the building, God changed the **language** of the different nationalities involved, not the races.

In Chapter Two we talked about how this problem was perpetuated by hate groups like the KKK for example, who taught that God created the races differently and intended for them to remain separated. This probably was the beginning of racism as we know it today. The hypocrisy of this practice continued to grow worse with age as all habits do!

Out of this grew the fallacy and myth of the racial inferiority of blacks, as opposed to the racial superiority of whites. Because many people initially believed the teaching of the KKK (Ku Klux Klan), it gave rise to the perpetuation of the problem to such an extent that **Jim Crow laws were** originated, and proved to be the apex of segregation, and the flawed propaganda of the separate, but equal treatment of the races. The separation was separate, but never equal!

This is where the distrust with higher education in the black community started. Since the colleges and universities were all owned by white people, it was initially viewed as a way to further indoctrinate and assimilate blacks, by teaching them the philosophy and the way of thinking by the white society. Here is where the notion of being "whitewashed" in college came from.

This is primarily why we have the current dilemma of higher education and the integrity of black identity. It appears at first sight that this concern has some validity, but upon further examination it proves to be lacking. The argument that this notion is a cover up for black anger and apathy is talked about in the **critique of blackness.**

In Chapter Three we discussed the result of this crisis as being the birth of the black intellectual as being a **hybrid** being! He is a hybrid being because of his College degree, he is now too white to be black, and too black to be white. He doesn't fit in either world.

In Chapter Four, we saw how he is on the outside looking in on his own black community. In many ways he is now invisible because he doesn't act black or talk black anymore. Right or not, his critique of the black culture is ignored by his own people. If black intellectuals cannot critique his own, where will such al critique come from, certainly not from the white intellectual!

We examined how this perceived whitewashing is behind the black fallacy of the loss of "blackness" whatever that means. This term was critiqued thoroughly and found to be without real substance. This threat was determined to be a fallacy couched in racism.

We delineated what the real threat to blackness is. In this examination, we talked about the **nature** of blackness as really being the accepted lifestyle of blacks, especially in the inner city! It included the manner of dress often intended to be sloppy, repulsive music lyrics, the treatment of blacks by blacks, especially with black on black crime, murder, proliferation of drugs, rates of incarceration of young black males, etc. This is the kind of **positive criticism** that blacks need to be exposed to.

In Chapter Five, there was also the discussion about the black intellectual in the white community. He is accepted by some if he does doesn't talk too black or militantly, does not wear dread locks if he's not an entertainer, etc. It is made covertly clear, that although he is a college graduate, when it comes to big business, he is still only a black man with a college degree, who will only go so far up the corporate ladder.

In Chapter Six we discussed in detail what would be necessary to fix this problem. I called upon the collective wisdom of two white scholars to help me with this solution, in order that it does not appear entirely as my own solution. In this chapter we examined the role that the black male needs to play in all this, after all, this is his hand that has been dealt so will he play the hand or fold?

We are solely responsible for allowing this dilemma to reach the point that it has, because of our lacking to fully understand that this problem is completely a black one. We are the ones struggling to come to grips with looking negatively at how a college degree affects us a people, and cause such negativity among us. If this is ever to change, the impetus for it must be i**nitiated** by black folk. We are the ones who coined the phrase "whitewashing"

When the fact is analyzed why the black culture has lagged behind in the ongoing positive changes that have taken place in the last fifty years, we discover that the same self defeatist attitudes that have plagued us still exist today, like the "crabs in the barrel syndrome". We are still a very much divided and immature culture. Being whitewashed because we go to college is only one example of this immaturity. The out of control killing of each other is another example, especially since the white man is no longer our biggest enemy. That distinction now is ours and ours alone!

To help understand why this phenomenon exists in our culture, I referred to the wisdom of Harold Brown for his explanation of **Static and Dynamic** change, as they are played out in the black community. When the change is static for instance, nothing of essence really changes over time. This is evident for example, in the way that college students continue to act out in our black universities even today.

We talked about what criteria necessary to instigate the changes needed in order to eliminate these impediments. The motivation for change was examined very closely in order to pinpoint the necessary ingredients of such. One of the primary items found was the need to establish **disequilibrium** in our ways of thinking. In short, this involves the disturbance of our comfort zones, thus creating a sense of unsettlement and discomfort. It is only when they are disturbed do we see the need to develop new ones.

There is also a role that white society must play in creating an environment for change to take place as well. These problems of higher education do not exist without cause. These causes are traced to the historical practices of discrimination against blacks by whites. Therefore, it is also incumbent upon white society to help in making such changes by creating **disequilibrium** of their own comfort zones.

Blacks have a significant role to play at this point, because they must be willing to accept sincere overtures of peace offered by whites. In doing this, they are also allowing themselves to further the positive changes taking place in our society, without continually lamenting about what is wrong. They must be willing to give credit where credit is due.

This the only real way to ensure that the gains made recently between blacks and whites continue. However, the breaking down of these barriers will not be accomplished by mere social interaction. A much more extraordinary means need to take place. In order for this occur, Divine Intervention must play a role.

Harold Brown and Erich Fromm both allude to this reality in two distinctly different ways, while essentially saying the same thing. Brown refers to the breaking down of these long standing racial divisions fueled by racial hatred, cannot be closed once they are opened without the Amalgamation of rapid interbreeding. This practice will eventually produce a blur of physical distinctions, where one is not readily identified as belonging to a certain race or nationality.

This will tend to create a more cohesive and tranquil nature in human relationships where racial lines become less and less a factor. We can see this happening today when the children of mixed marriages are seen. They are beautiful kids, whether we want to admit It or not. My son is married to a German girl and they have given me three gorgeous Grand Sons of a mixed color, neither black nor white. Brown's observation made over fifty years ago appears to be prophetic.

Fromm on the other hand points to what he calls "**automaton Conformity.**" This is what he refers to as a society that is universally on **one** accord (not to be confused with one mind), mutually committed to a common cause agreed upon by all.

This means that individuals must be willing to give up a portion of their Self Identity and autonomy, and essentially creating an automated society dedicated to eradicating past ills and sins. This way of thinking is completely foreign to the way that humans think, and thus leads to the conclusion that Divine Intervention of some sort will be needed.

Brown and Fromm frame the solution by suggesting that only the Amalgamation of rapid interbreeding, and the commitment of every individual to the automaton of a common desired goal, both of which I affirm wholeheartedly, is man's only other alternative.

This summary is not to be considered as all inclusive, but rather as means of seeing the problem and surmising a possible solution.

A FINAL WORD

The assessment of the dilemma presented in this writing, could only have come from the hands of a black man who has several college degrees, and has lived and continues to live in the throes of this dilemma **firsthand**, and still is a black American and always will be. In part, this is an exposition of black life and culture that no white man could have written beyond mere empathy and speculation.

There are positive criticisms and critiques presented here that only a black could dare to propagate without being accused of being condescending and racist! Even though, the reality is that there will be blacks that will consider this to be a sellout and Uncle Tom like. Be that as it may, blacks must learn to be introspective and Self Critical in order to move on!

Anyone who reads this work, and has his or her own theories and dispositions about this matter, by all means write and explain them, because there is a tremendous thirst for your wisdom and insights about this.

CONCLUSION

The primary thesis of this writing is three fold. First, is the attempt to **preserve** history by alluding to its importance in the framing of our lives. This is crucial for enhancing the understanding of those who have no firsthand knowledge of the role that these have played in determining our lives today. This is why it is so important for parents to teach these lessons of history to their children. It is an absolute truism that if we don't learn from history, we are doomed to repeat it!

Secondly, is the attempt to **inform** the world today of the lessons learned from history. This is probably the greatest need of our young people today. Our youth to a great extent live in a social vacuum when it comes to understanding why certain things exist as they are. Here is where parents today are selling their children short.

One prime example is the importance of this type of education in historical documents during the celebration of black history month, where videos and documentaries show the ghastly racial turmoil of the 60's and 70's to our youth.

Last but certainly not least, is to provide **inspiration for** a better tomorrow based upon what we have learned from the past. History is not a static and dead discipline, but a dynamic and live reality, because we are who we are today because of it. We are living history because there is only the **present** moment which is the here and now, and as soon as that is said, it becomes **immediate** history. We are now the sum total of the past, present and what we will be tomorrow!

Tomorrow is determined by the choices that we make today. In order to solve the current dilemmas that exist today, we must learn to use history as a possible solution to them in order to bring about a better tomorrow.